The
Nut Magnet

Do Some of Us Have a
Sign That Reads:
*"Hey Crazy People, Tell
Me Your Life Story?"*

Ron Lomax

RKLL Publishers
2543 Wildcat Creek Blvd
Springdale, AR 72762

ISBN-13: 978-0692026595
ISBN-10: 0692026592

Scripture is taken from the New International Version 2011 of the Holy Bible, by permission.

DEDICATION

*This book is dedicated
to all the men and women
who faithfully proclaim
the Good News of Jesus Christ.*

*How beautiful are the feet
of those who bring good news!*
Romans 10:15

CONTENTS

Acknowledgments 9

Introduction 11

1 **They Say The Fun Is In Getting There** 13

Into the Wild Blue Yonder 13

2 **Leherutshe, Bophuthatswana** 19

First Thanksgiving 19

Language School 21

Water From the Well 24

Lesotho Mountains 27

Spiritual Lesson Learned 30

Don't Get Sick 33

Post Office 34

Snake Stories 36

3 **GaRankuwa, Bophuthatswana** 39

Let the Riots Begin 39

New Addition 44

The Hearse 46

African Culture 49

Youth Camps 51

Afrikaner People Group 55

Afrikaner Good Samaritans 56

Stalking Lions 60

God Heals the Sick 61

4 Johannesburg – Soweto 65

Thusong Baptist Center 65

Stolen at Gunpoint 69

Church Start 72

Foolish Builder 75

Soup Kitchen 78

Waiting for the Darkness 80

Democracy Comes to South Africa 83

Missionary Nuts 84

Otter Trail Hostel 90

Kruger National Park 91

Furloughs 93

5 Beautiful Cape Town 97

Seminary Days 98

Sad Times 102

Sports Evangelism 104

Journeymen 109

Fireworks 112

Speaking of Gangs . . . 114

Seal Island 116

Deep Sea Fishing 117

Basketball Association 120

TV Basketball Commentators 122

VETS Tourney 124

Conference in the African Bush 127

6 Other Country Travels 135

Botswana: Not Another Fishing Trip! 135

Mauritius Anniversary 137

Australia, New Zealand, Hawaii 139

Other Country Travels 141

Conclusion 143

About the Author 147

ACKNOWLEDGMENTS

I wish to give special thanks:

To the people, *and especially all the nuts*,
who have made this book possible.

To all the missionaries we worked with through
the International Mission Board, SBC, and
specifically those whom we worked beside
in the country of South Africa.

To my wife, Karen, and our children, Braden,
Kaylan, and Kelsey, for allowing me to share
our lifetime experiences with the world.

To a good friend of ours, Brenda Wright,
for her editorial precision and advice.

To all those people in the many churches, camps, and
conferences where we have told our stories who kept
saying, *"Why don't you write these things down?*

INTRODUCTION

Nut, *noun*
1. a. An indehiscent, hard-shelled, one-
        loculated, one-seeded fruit, such as
        an acorn or hazelnut.
    b. A seed borne within a fruit having
       a hard shell, as in the peanut,
       almond, or walnut.
    c. The kernel of any of these.
2. *Slang*
    a. A crazy or eccentric person.
    b. An enthusiast; a buff: *a movie nut.*
3. *Informal.* A difficult endeavor or problem:
    Painting the closet was a tough nut to crack.

… and the winner is definition #2a!
I once read a quote, author unknown, that said, "I
look at my friends and think to myself, 'Where did I
meet these crazy people?' But then I think 'What
would I do without them?'"

11

I have a good friend who tells the greatest stories about all the people he has come across throughout his life. I commented on his stories one day, about all the weird and crazy people he's come across, and he made the statement that he must be a "nut magnet."

Then he stared at me, probably thinking about the nuts I also encounter in life, and made the statement that, actually, we are both nut magnets. So, I guess I'm actually Nut Magnet #2.

Why do some people attract nuts?
Do some of us have a sign that reads, *"Hey crazy people, tell me your life story?"*

I'm not even sure whether its referring to the people we meet along the way or to me as an individual, but if the shoe fits . . . I don't know, you decide.

This book speaks about our family's missionary journey throughout the country of South Africa for 18½ years. It talks about all the nuts we met along the way and some of the nutty situations in which we found ourselves. Some names of people have been used and some have not, to protect the guilty!

It also speaks about a lot of experiences and friends we met along the way. And, as we live life, God shows us His truth in everything, so enjoy the spiritual nuggets throughout!

1 THEY SAY THE FUN IS IN GETTING THERE

"For I know the plans I have for you,' declares the Lord, 'plans to prosper you and not to harm you, plans to give you hope and a future. Then you will call upon me and come and pray to me, and I will listen to you. You will seek me and find me when you seek me with all your heart.'"
Jeremiah 29:11-13.

Into the Wild Blue Yonder

I'm not sure exactly where our journey to the international mission field began, but I'll pick it up when Karen and I were in seminary in New Orleans and we decided to work at Ridgecrest Baptist Conference Center in North Carolina during the summer of 1981. We had met while on summer staff at Ridgecrest in 1977, so going back to work another summer felt right. While there that summer, we had jobs that allowed us to attend many of the worship services during the different themed weeks. It was during "Foreign Missions Week" that God directed our attention toward missions specifically. Dr. Keith Parks, then President of the Foreign Mission Board (later named the International Mission Board) was the featured speaker during the worship times. During one of his sermons we felt God's hand leading us forward one night to speak to a counselor about the possibility of overseas missionary work. We agreed that we would speak to someone from this mission board later, after we returned to seminary, in order for us to decide if our future would be in missionary service.

My wife and I firmly believe in living on mission with God. That is our calling as Christians, to be like Christ. And, He was always on mission with His Father. To live missionally is to live sent.

"Again Jesus said, 'Peace be with you! As the Father has <u>sent</u> me, I am <u>sending</u> you.'" John 20:21.
"How, then, can they call on the one they have not believed in? And how can they believe in the one of whom they have not heard? And how can they hear without someone preaching to them? And how can anyone preach unless they are <u>sent</u>? As it is written: 'How beautiful are the feet of those who bring good news!'" Romans 10:14-15.

Through seminary and two church staff jobs later, it was in 1987 that we spoke again to the Foreign Mission Board about serving overseas as missionaries. We accepted an assignment in Uganda to be Youth Workers in the Kampala area. However, this wasn't to become our real assignment because while at Glorietta Baptist Conference Center in New Mexico to be commissioned, our assignment changed, and we changed countries. Much political unrest was happening in Uganda and the Board asked us to pray about another assignment in Bophuthatswana, South Africa, as Baptist Convention Youth Workers. Bophuthatswana was one of several Homelands in South Africa where the African black populations were made to live in apartheid South Africa. We couldn't pronounce it, but we felt right about this and accepted that assignment. I resigned my church ministry position in Poplar Bluff, MO, and we traveled to Richmond, VA, to go through the Missionary Learning Center, and then on to our assignment. Upon completion seven weeks later, we were headed for South Africa in November, 1987.

Now, in all our years of travel since then, I have never experienced flights like those that took these two young American parents of two children under two years old to South Africa. Braden was 21 months old and Kaylan was 6 months old when we boarded that big plane in Atlanta, GA. I don't know how old they were when we finally deplaned in Johannesburg, but I think Karen and I had aged five years! I guess I should have looked at the Great Commission more clearly, because it does say in the King James Version, *"And LO I am with you always . . ."* Jesus didn't mention anything about up *HIGH*!

We left the USA, headed for South Africa without a South African visa, mistake number one (which is okay now, but in those days, you didn't do that). One of our missionaries (nut) in Johannesburg had told us to come on, he would take care of it. I know, I know, but at that time I trusted missionaries! We left Atlanta and headed for Amsterdam and a 13-hour layover, which I never got to enjoy or rest with my family, as I was at the airport trying to talk the airline into flying us on to Africa when I wasn't in possession of a South African visa. In the end, they agreed to fly us to South Africa and then on to Botswana if the visa didn't come through. *Great.*

We flew from Amsterdam to Nairobi, Kenya, for a layover. We got off the plane to walk around and were met by soldiers with AK-47 guns, not a pleasant sight for these Americans who had never traveled outside of the USA. The soldiers were just patrolling the airport facilities. We got back on the plane, we could walk later!

After about a 45-hour trip, we arrived in Johannesburg, South Africa, literally exhausted. Kaylan didn't sleep well on the plane so Karen ended up walking the plane for many hours. All that, plus, just the fact that a man who is 6'3" tall doesn't fit well into economy seating, made for a long, long trip. We were met in Johannesburg by airport officials, who had pulled our luggage off and loaded it on trolleys, and wanted to take us to the Botswana flight because, guess what, we didn't have South African visas! I explained to them about a man *(nut)* who told us to come on, he would take care of it. But, after many intercom pages, this man couldn't be found. We were about 5 minutes from being taken to the Botswana flight when a customs official came through the door

with our South African visas in his shirt pocket. He had taken a break and forgot he had them! The missionary (nut) came through! Would we have flown to Botswana? I don't know, because my inclination at the time was to catch a plane back to the USA and never to step foot in Africa again.
God, are You sure about this?

Since our visa was only a 24-hour visa to be renewed in South Africa, we couldn't spend the night at the Missionary Guest House in Johannesburg. No, we had to drive three hours to the Language School after leaving the airport. The School Director and his wife, missionaries (nuts!), were there with the group at the airport to meet us, and once we got the entire luggage packed away in two vehicles and a trailer, the Director asked me if I wanted to drive. One look at me looking at the Toyota midget car with the steering wheel on the right and the other cars driving on the left side of the road indicated to the Director that maybe that wasn't a good idea. He drove. What a trip from American to Africa, and what a great story for later on.

We jokingly like to tell people that was the trip from "you know where," but looking back we could see how God was preparing us for His service in a new place, with a new culture of strange languages and weird customs. God's faithfulness is new every morning.

"Because of the Lord's great love we are not consumed, for his compassions never fail. They are new every morning; great is your faithfulness."

Lamentations 3:22-23

There is a poem based on these verses from Lamentations, written in the early 1920s by a life insurance agent named Thomas Chisholm. He sent the poem to a friend who set it to music. It has become one of the best-loved hymns of this century, "Great Is Thy Faithfulness." The hymn writer wrote these words about God: "Morning by morning new mercies I see. Thou changest not, Thy compassions they fail not, as Thou hast been Thou forever wilt be." According to Thomas Chisholm, there was no special or dramatic circumstance surrounding the writing of this hymn; he simply penned the lines from his impressions about God's faithfulness gleaned from reading the Bible.

Since mission work is a large part of our lives, here are a few quotes about missions which have become favorites:

"The Bible is not the basis of missions; mission is the basis of the Bible." – Ralph Winter
"The missional church is made up of missionaries who are playing the big game every day. They live their lives with the idea they are on a mission trip. On a mission trip, people focus on the work of God around them, alert to the Spirit's prompting, usually serving people in very tangible ways, often in ways that involve some sacrifice or even discomfort."
Reggie McNeal, Missional Renaissance (Jossey-Bass, 2009)
"Any church that is not seriously involved in helping fulfill the Great Commission has forfeited its biblical right to exist." – Oswald J. Smith

2 LEHERUTSHE, BOPHUTHATSWANA
(Lay-ha-root-se, Bo-poo-tat-swana)

First Thanksgiving

Since we arrived in South Africa a week before Thanksgiving, we traveled with another missionary couple several hours south to another missionary family's home to celebrate the holiday. There were 15 adult missionaries there along with six kids. Four of the couples had been on the mission field for some time and were considerably older than we were. The missionary host family was older than us, had four kids, and had already spent several terms on the field. He was a veterinarian who was teaching at the local agricultural college. The rest of the group were a young couple who was finishing up a two-year Journeyman assignment and a single male Journeyman.

Since Karen and I were still brand new on the mission field and still under some jetlag from all that traveling, I don't remember a lot of what we did that day, except eat Thanksgiving dinner. We stayed two nights and our daughter was sick most of that time. One night, the younger ones (us included!) decided to stay up longer and watch a couple movies that someone had brought along. It was approximately 9:00 p.m.

Did I mention there was a pretty big generational gap between the families there? We were moving the TV and VCR out of the living room because one of the older couples was sleeping in that room. We were moving these things to the large hallway so the movie wouldn't bother anyone. The older man who was sleeping in the living room came over to us and asked, "What are you doing?" We told him. He asked us if we didn't think that was rude because the host family might want to go to bed, after all, it was almost nine o'clock. One of the younger men said, "Are you nuts?" Fortunately, our host, the veterinarian, came up and heard the conversation and announced, "Hey, I'm watching the movie too, no problem." So, all was well. Some went to bed and others of us watched several movies well into the night.

(Old nut missionaries!)

Language School

Now the real fun begins. The language school is in a "location" near some villages. We began learning the Setswana language and culture – these two Americans who had never been outside of the USA, or had ever studied another language. I knew southeast Missouri English and Karen knew Georgia southern, which I always considered two different languages anyway. If you've ever heard missionaries speak of language learning, then you've heard of some pretty goofy and funny mistakes, and we made all of them.

There are many terminology differences between American English and South African English. And, when those differences are put into a tribal language, it gets *very* interesting.

Just take the parts of a car – the hood is the bonnet and the trunk is the boot. Under the bonnet is the motor, not the engine. You indicate with the indicator, you don't turn on the blinker. The glove box is the cubby hole and the windshield is the windscreen. And, best of all, you don't honk your horn, you hoot your hooter!

So, you put your bag in the boot and get in your car and start the motor. Make sure the bonnet is closed or that could cause an accident. You get some gum out of the cubby hole and look through the windscreen to make sure it's safe to proceed. If something gets in your way, hoot your hooter! Now, drive to the second robot and turn left into the petrol station. A robot is a traffic signal light and petrol powers the motor, not gas. Gas is something you cook with.

Sometime after being in language study, I got to drive to the "petrol" station to fill up, using my newly acquired Setswana terminology. As I was pulling out of the school, the language director hopped into my "kombi" (van) to ride along. *Big mistake, never take the language school director with you when you are practicing your language skills.*

We drove up to the pump and I looked out my window and told the attendant to "fill up my tank" in Setswana. He looked at me oddly and asked me to repeat myself. I did. Then, the attendant *and the school director* began giggling. Well, my thought was this: "They know one another and are trying to throw off this new language student into thinking he isn't saying it right." So, I just got a little louder and said to him once again, "Fill up my tank" in my newly acquired Setswana. Now, they went from giggling to laughing. The school director asked me, "Ron, what do you think you said to him?" I told him what I thought I said. He said, "Well, you actually told him to vomit into your tank!" I looked in my side mirror and saw that he was actually filling my tank with petrol, so everything was okay.

When I got back to the Language School and sat down with our language teacher, I told her I had made a mistake at the petrol station. She asked what I had done *this time*, indicating that I had made a few mistakes before. I told her what I told the station attendant and she just put her hands over her face and said, "You told him to vomit!" I said, "Yes, I understand that now, but what was I supposed to say?" She repeated the word I was supposed to say, which means "to fill." Well, to me it sounded just like the word for "vomit!" If you spell them on paper, one word has an "l" in the middle the other one does not have, so it all depended on the inflection you put on the letter as to which thing it meant, to vomit or to fill. So, we practiced the rest of the afternoon what to say at the petrol station.

I learned my lesson. The next time I pulled into the station, I politely said to the attendant, "Full tank, please," in very slow English. He understood every word!

There was much to learn in those early days. About half-way through language school, we had to go to a village and do a week live-in with a local family. As Americans though, we take about half the school with us as we go. With us, we had our language teacher, Mme (pronounced "May," a word which meant Mrs. or Ms.) Bertha, her 2-year-old son Ompile, our nanny and our two kids, the young single missionary Journeyman who was with us at Thanksgiving, and another young man from our church in Missouri who was out visiting us for his summer, our winter. We stayed with a very nice family who had simple electricity in their house but no running water. They had to go to the village well to draw water and kept it in large barrels at the house.

Water From the Well

One day I decided that we three men would take care of getting the water from the well, which, according to South African culture, was the woman's job. *And one more mistake: As a man, don't try to take on the woman's job.* The lady of the house was preparing us for the job. She brought the wheel barrow and two very large, empty, round plastic jugs which fit into the wheel barrow. Since there were three of us, me and the two young guys with us, I asked her if we could take a third jug in order to get more water. She said "You won't be able to carry three, only two will fit into the wheel barrow, so take two." But, we were three healthy, strong, American men, we could surely carry three, so we took three. She was laughing as we walked away. *(Nuts!)*

She had pointed and told us where the well was located, and said, "Go that way, it's just here." That was when I started learning what "just here" meant. It was like another of their sayings concerning "now." They say, "Now," "Just now," and "Now, now." "Now" means sometime in the next couple days. "Just now" means maybe today. And "Now, now" means in the next hour or so. So, "just here" wasn't necessarily close. We pushed that wheel barrow and carried those three jugs quite a distance, across fields, down through a dry creek bed, up the bank and across another field to get to the village well. There were two women drawing water when we arrived, doing the job of a woman.

After watching them to figure out how to draw the

water, we filled up our three jugs and then tried to figure out how to carry them in the wheel barrow, in which only two of them fit. Plus, one jug was much too heavy to carry very far, apart from the wheel barrow, which we didn't realize when they were empty. *Yes, I remember hearing her laugh as we walked away from the house.*

Well, this scene was becoming pretty funny to the two ladies at the well. Just the sight of three white American men trying to carry three jugs of water, when everyone knows the wheel barrow is only made for two, was more than they could handle. By the time we finally walked away from the well, there were about 12 ladies at the well, who had been called by the other two to come and watch. I'm glad we could make their day. Who needs television?

We decided to put two jugs in the wheel barrow and to carry the third jug just far enough away from the well that they wouldn't see us pour out most of the water from the third jug. Then, we struggled back to where we had come from to get the water back to the house. When we were just a short distance from the house, we evenly divided the water from the two jugs back into all three jugs to show we could bring water in three jugs from the well to the house. The lady of the house was pretty impressed! But, we also knew she would find out the truth soon enough, word seemed to travel quickly in that village! *(Nuts!)*

We had done so well with the water that the lady of the house asked me what I wanted for our group to eat. I had heard people talk about sorghum porridge and thought that would be something sweet and good to eat. So, I asked for sorghum porridge. *Just one more mistake. A lot of food in South Africa looks like it would be sweet only to bite into it and find that it doesn't taste like it looks.* They put the sorghum into a pot of water, with I'm not sure what else, and cook it for a long time. Then, they let it sit the rest of the day and turn sour, hence their other name for it, *"sour porridge."* So, this is what she served our group that night, along with some green things and a pumpkin dish. Needless to say, our group was not very happy with me. It is the custom to eat everything on your plate to show good manners so we ate it all. She came to the table and asked how I liked it. I had to say it was great to show respect, so she gave me another plate full. We had some of that for several days afterwards since she had made such a large pot of it. I found that if you put enough sugar and milk on something, it's not all bad. *(Nut!)*

Lesotho Mountains

We had opportunity to travel down to a land-locked country within the borders of South Africa called Lesotho. The Sotho culture and language spoken there was very similar to the Setswana language we were learning. We travelled down there with some missionary friends who were our Language School Directors and were eventually planning to transfer to Lesotho.

We also had the young man, Scott, our friend from our home in Missouri, who was visiting us for his American summer, which was still our South African winter. The other missionaries had arranged for all of us to stay at a small hotel in the mountains outside the capital city of Maseru for two nights. They stayed in one room and our family, plus Scott, stayed in another room.

Since this was the South African winter and we were in the mountains, snow was everywhere and it was cold. Most places in South Africa do not have central air or heat, and this hotel was that kind of place. There was a very small coal-burning stove in the room for heat and a very small bucket of coal standing by the stove. In the bathroom there was a huge, rusted water heater hanging over the bathtub. So when you were in the bath your mind was on whether or not that water heater was going to fall or not. I guess that made people take quick baths while using very little hot water.

Well, by about three o'clock in the morning, that

bucket of coal was gone and the fire was waning. We were starting to get *pretty cold* in that room. Scott was sleeping in a bed with our son and we were in a bed with our daughter, with everyone freezing.

Scott and I decided we were going to have to go outside in the snow and darkness and find some wood. Have you ever gone outside in the snow and darkness and tried to find wood? Yeah, it was all hidden under the snow! So while I tried to keep the fire burning with whatever I could find, Scott went outside to find wood. Sometime later there was a knock on the door. It was Scott pulling what looked like a whole tree through the door. We had leaves and snow and dirt all over that floor as we broke off limbs and sticks to shove into the stove for fire and warmth. Just surviving took up most of the remainder of the night! Those survivalist shows on TV have nothing on us!

The next morning we went to the restaurant for breakfast, having gotten very little sleep during the night because we had to work to survive the cold. The other missionary couple was there, all cheery-eyed, looking like they got a great night of sleep. They looked at us and he asked how our night was. Bad question dude!

I told them our night's story of why we got very little sleep. There's nothing like waking up freezing with the fire going out and having to go out in the dead of winter to find firewood. This guy just started laughing, I thought about punching him but remembered we were missionaries. *Not really.*

He shared these words of wisdom, "Why didn't you just take your bucket down to the basement and get more coal? There is a whole truckload down there." *Did anyone TELL us there was coal in the basement? No!* How would we know that unless someone told us? Were there any signs in the room telling us to go to the basement for more coal? *No! (Nutcases!)*

He said that since we now knew where to find more coal the next night would be better. I thought of all that debris on the floor in our room from our night's labor. I told him that we would not be staying another night in this ice hotel, we were driving down the mountain to the capital city and finding a nice warm hotel to stay in that night. And, we did.

We ended up staying in a great, clean, modern for Lesotho standards, hotel. There was a bathtub with no water heater in sight and an air conditioning-heating unit under the window. What luxury we enjoyed, thank you Lord.
(Satisfied nuts!)

Spiritual Lesson Learned

A great spiritual lesson learned while in language school came on a day in the bush with the shepherds. The missionary vet who we had spent that first Thanksgiving with was now at the language school learning some Setswana, even though they had been on the field for some time. One day he was going to meet the shepherds out in the bush and help them with a sheep dip, and I went along. I had grown up on a farm which raised crops and cattle, so I thought this would be interesting. The dip area is a large concrete tank in the ground with fenced pens on each side, and ramps leading down in and up out of the dip tank. They fill the entry pen with sheep, push them into the dip solution in the tank, swirl them around in there for a few minutes to let the dip solution kill all the bugs in their wool, and then they open a gate and let the sheep walk up the ramp to the holding pen on the other side. A few minutes after that, they open the outer gate and the sheep come out into open ground.

I was watching all this about to take place as the vet was explaining it to me. When we arrived, there were no sheep around, just the guys preparing the dip solution in the tank. Then, herds of sheep started coming over the hills with their shepherds. Remember, there are no fences out there. As I watched this, I started to wonder how this was going to go down. Several herds of sheep would be put into the first pen together. Then they would get wet and come out the other side. If you think all sheep look alike when they are dry, try looking at them when they are all wet. Identical. I was thinking, there may be some fights breaking out in the end because the shepherds wouldn't know which sheep belonged to whom, and the herds would get mixed up. I thought one shepherd who brought 12 sheep would take back 10 while one who brought 30 would take back 35. This, I thought, is going to cause a big fight! This is going to be exciting!

One word: *Amazing!* You know how you get goose bumps when you see a spiritual lesson lived out in front of your eyes? Well, that was the case here. When the last gate was opened and the wet sheep came out into the open, an amazing thing happened. The sheep would come out of the gate and stop. They would lift their heads, and listen. To what? They were listening for their shepherd's voice. One shepherd on the hillside was calling out in words. Another shepherd was whistling. Another shepherd was singing. Another shepherd was clapping his hands. And the sheep would listen, and then head straight for their shepherd's voice!

"When he has brought out all his own, he goes on ahead of them, and his sheep follow him because they know his voice. But they will never follow a stranger; in fact, they will run away from him because they do not recognize a stranger's voice." John 10:4-5.
"I am the good shepherd; I know my sheep and my sheep know me – just as the Father knows me and I know the Father – and I lay down my life for the sheep." John 10:14-15.
"My sheep listen to my voice; I know them, and they follow me." John 11:27.

I got to see these Scriptures lived out before me that day, and it was simply amazing.

Don't Get Sick

Visiting the doctor's office at the hospital was another adventure while at the "location." There were three doctors at our local hospital. One was a German doctor whose wife we had met when she had taken some classes with us. Through her we met him and would see them occasionally around the location. So, if we got sick, that is who we would want to see.

The South African money system is called Rand. One American dollar at that time was equal to about two Rand ($1 = R2). When you went to the hospital, you paid 50 Rand cents ($.25) and took the next seat. That money would pay for the doctor visit and any medication you needed to take with you. There were seats lined up all the way around a very large waiting room, the size of half a basketball court. Every time someone went in to see the next available doctor, everyone got up and moved over one seat. It was a social time for the people, even though they were sick with whatever was ailing them. I'm not sure how many extra germs one was able to pick up as they moved from seat to seat. It was definitely an all morning affair.

After doing this one day and talking about the experience with our language teacher, she informed us on how to do it the next time. She told us if we paid two Rand (R2 or $1.00) we could go to the front of the line, bypassing all the germs. And, they told us, if we paid R5 ($2.50), we could also choose our doctor. So, after that, we always paid R5 and saw our German doctor friend.

Post Office

One day, our teacher told us about another custom. When you get into a queue (line), you stand up against the person in front of you so no one can break the queue. I felt a little uneasy about this, being an American, and enjoying my personal space.

One day I went to the little Post Office at the location. I got into the queue and left personal space between me and the person in front of me. When I looked around at something and turned back, there was a little man in front of me, in my personal space. It kind of caught me off guard.

I tapped him on the shoulder and he looked around and up at me. I told him this is my space, his space would be at the end of the queue, about 12 people back, and I pointed at the end of the queue. He said, "No, this space was empty." I told him that space was not empty, it was my space, and he would need to go to the end of the queue. He said again it was his and it was quite obvious he wasn't going to move.

The others in the queue were enjoying this, probably wondering what the American was going to do next. I gently put my hands on his shoulders, sort of lifted him up a bit, and slowly propelled him to the end of the queue. I put him there and said, "Now, here is your space. That (pointing to my space), is my space. You stay here." So, I went back to my space.

At this, the others in the queue broke out in applause and laughter because that was the best show they'd seen in a while. Crazy missionary! I would see the little guy around town every once-in-awhile and he would point at me and laugh. *(Nuts!)*

"There is a time for everything, and a season for every activity under heaven . . . A time to weep and a time to laugh." Ecclesiastes 3:1, 4.

Snake Stories

I guess every missionary in Africa has one or more snake stories and we're no different. Once, while driving over a dusty road, I noticed a large stick in the road. As I got closer, I veered to one side of the road to not run over the large stick. When I got even with the "stick" and stopped beside it, the stick was actually a large cobra, which coiled itself beside the car and lifted his head up to look at me through my much closed window. I hoped he couldn't break glass because I'm really not a fan of snakes, so I stepped on the "petrol" and drove on!

Our house at the language school had tile floors and we kept the doors and windows open due to the fact that we didn't have air conditioning. The doorways had a type of screen door on them, but with several inches of openness at the bottom, they served to keep only large things out. One day our daughter, Kaylan, was flying around the house in her walker. The walker was a South African model, no wheels, just really sharp, plastic, round discs on the bottom. We were in another room when she went into the living room, then we heard her scream and the walker made a noise like hitting the wall. I actually thought she had sailed out the front door. When I ran into the living room, I noticed 2 small oblong pieces of something on the floor by the walker. Kaylan had run over a snake that had come into the house and cut it into two pieces. One more African snake had bitten the dust . . .

"The Lord protects you; the Lord is a shelter right by your side.

The sun will not strike you by day or the moon by night. The Lord will protect you from all harm. The Lord will protect your coming and going both now and forever." Psalm 121:5-8

I went backpacking with some of the other missionary men a couple times a year. On one of these early hikes, at one of the overnight huts, there was a large poster on the wall with pictures of many, many different kinds of snakes. The caption at the bottom said something like this, "Keep an eye out along the trail for snakes. But, don't worry, South Africa only has eight deadly snakes." Are you serious? Only eight? How many does America have? Growing up in Missouri, I think we only had to worry about three kinds of poisonous snakes. But, needless to say, I watched every step!

One of our constant prayers as we lived on the mission field was that God would keep us safe and protected. For some reason, that prayer was more of a felt need living overseas. And, He continues to fulfill that prayer each day.

3 GARANKUWA, BOPHUTHATSWANA
(Ha-ran-ku-wa)

Let the Riots Begin

After language school, we had a house built and moved over to a place called GaRankuwa, Bophuthatswana. The population was approximately one million and we were the only white family in the area where we lived. We had great neighbors who watched over us and protected us.

Apartheid was the government policy at the time in South Africa: Apartheid [*uh*-**pahrt**-heyt] *noun*
1. A rigid policy of segregation of the nonwhite population.
2. Any system or practice that separates people according to race, caste, etc.

One of many draw-backs of Apartheid was that it caused the different races of people to fight against their own. The Bophu people fought against their own government because they felt it was put in place by the white Apartheid South African government. One day, a riot was going to break out in our area, and we knew nothing about it until we were caught right in the middle of it.

That morning we got up as usual and I drove the 20 kilometers (12 miles) into South Africa to take our son to a day care center. I drove back home and began working in the yard. A few hours later, we started to hear and see helicopters flying over and then soon afterward, horns began honking (actually, in South Africa, this would be called "hooters hooting"), and then blasts that we thought were fireworks shooting off. I got in my kombi (van) and drove over a few kilometers near the government buildings to see what was happening.

As I was driving up the road with the government buildings in sight, a group of people jumped out onto the road and blocked my way. One man came up to my window and told me to get out of the kombi because they needed it. I told them, "This kombi belongs to the church and you can't have it." He said once more that they were taking the kombi. They said they needed it because some babies and mothers needed to go to the hospital because they had been tear-gassed by the police. I told them I would take the babies to the hospital if they would show me the way. I also figured that this was the only way I was going to keep my kombi! So, one of the men hopped in the passenger seat and we started off down the road. We came to a blockade made of round concrete culverts across the road, and he leaned out the window and shouted something I didn't understand, but basically he was telling whoever was listening that I was a comrade and to move the blockade. People came from seemingly nowhere, moved the blockade, and then put it back in place after we drove through. All this time, I could see that the police at the government building were shooting across the road at the people who were in return, throwing petrol bombs and rocks back at them. It was definitely a place I didn't need or want to be at that present time.

We stopped in front of a house and three moms with babies came out and got into the van with me. I followed directions and took them to another house where a clinic was located and dropped them there. It was time I got back home, so as I was pulling away, another woman ran up to me and asked me if I could take the 12-year old boy she had with her out of that area. I told her I could take him to my house and he could get home later. I was in the process of telling her my address, and she interrupted me and said she knew where I lived and told me I lived in Unit 6. I guess when you are the *different color* family, everyone knows where you live. At that same time, something hit the road behind my van and rolled underneath. It was a tear gas canister, and I had my first experience with tear gas. I wondered why everyone else was wearing cloth over their noses and why they kept dipping them in buckets of water. Now I knew, and it was not pleasant, with the tears, you can't see anything and it burns. Needless to say, we got out of there fast and I drove quickly back the few miles to home.

As we watched the helicopters come and go and heard all the noise around, I remembered that I had to go back to the day care and pick up our son. So, I waited as long as possible and then drove out. I passed cars burning beside the road. I also passed telephone poles torn down and laid across the road, so had to drive on the shoulder of the road to pass. I finally got to the day care and then dreaded the drive back home. When we got to the border between South Africa and Bophu, there was a South African Police roadblock. The police told me there was no one going in or coming out. I explained to him that I lived in there and had to get to my family. Finally, he told me that if I insisted on going in, they would not be responsible for me and wanted to know why I would live someplace like that. I don't think he understood my answer: "This is where the Lord wants us to be." The drive back home took us past a burning bus and more debris that wasn't there earlier. Now, the Bophu army trucks were on the road, so I was really glad to get home without further incident.

When my neighbor lady heard about our day, she was upset with herself. She told us that she should have informed us what was going to go down that day because they knew. A few weeks later she came over on a Monday and told us that kind of thing was going to happen again on the weekend so we needed to take our kids the next weekend and go visit our friends in Johannesburg. She would take care of the house and feed the dog. We went away for the weekend and came back the following Monday. All was fine. She had looked after everything and the dog was happy. She even told me two men came to my gate on Saturday looking for Bibles and she told them to come back during the week.

*"God 'will give to each person according to what he has done.'
To those who by persistence in doing good seek glory, honor and
immortality, he will give eternal life. But for those who are self-
seeking and who reject the truth and follow evil, there will be
wrath and anger. There will be trouble and distress for every
human being who does evil: first for the Jew, then for the
Gentile; but glory, honor and peace for everyone who does good:
first for the Jew, then for the Gentile. For God does not show
favoritism."* Romans 2:6-11.

New Addition

Our youngest child, Kelsey, was born while we lived in GaRankuwa. She was born in Africa to American parents, so that makes her an African American! We lived a little distance from Pretoria where the hospital was, about a 40-minute drive, and barely made it on the day of delivery. The Afrikaans doctor just walked into the room to literally catch Kelsey coming out, so I asked him if we had to pay him for that. He didn't have much of a sense of humor! *(Doctor Nut!)*

Braden and Kaylan liked having Kelsey around because it gave them one more person for their church. They would play church in our Labrador's doghouse. In the village churches, after church, everyone would file out of the building, singing, forming a circle outside, and shaking hands with everyone before them as they then took their place in the circle. Then they would stand there and finish the song, then dismiss. So, after church in the doghouse, Braden would come out slapping his Bible, singing some song we'd never heard before, and take his place at the beginning of the circle. Then Kaylan would come out, doing the same thing, shake hands with Braden, then take her place in the circle. Kelsey would just follow suit, and believe it or not, Smokey, our Lab, would follow Kelsey and take his place in the circle! We even have video of this. We had to show it to the kids when they got older to prove to them they really did that!

Once, while on a trip to a wild-game park, we visited the lion cub enclosure where they could be petted.

While Kelsey, about 4 or 5 years old at the time, was petting an 8-week old cub, a 12-week old cub walked up behind her and bit her on the bum. Kelsey was not impressed with that lion and let him know it. She turned around and smacked him on the nose and told him, "No, no!" But, it made a great story in our next newsletter we sent to the USA, "MK (missionary kid) gets bitten by lion in Africa!" I think we got a call from my mom after that. *(Nut, grandmother.)*

The Hearse

One day our pastor from the village church came by and told us his father had died and the funeral would be on Saturday. We knew we needed to go but didn't want to tie up our whole Saturday, as funerals sometimes did in that culture. They would put up a large tent at the house and have the funeral there. It could last several hours. Next, they would go to the cemetery, where they would stay until the grave was covered by the men attending the funeral. Then, they would go back to the house and feed everyone in the village. One thing that irritated me during those early days when I was learning the culture, when I went anywhere, I was the taxi. It would take forever to deliver everyone (no GPS then) and then go home. But, that was because not many people had vehicles, and those who did had small cars or trucks, not vans, like the taxi drivers, and some missionaries, drove.

After the funeral at the house, the family would have hired city buses to go along with the few personal cars to provide transportation to and from the cemetery. To keep from being a taxi for the funeral, I decided to drive a very small truck (they call it a bakkie) that the mission owned and, *as God would have it*, was parked at my house. It would only hold two people up front! Finally, I would outsmart them.

We drove to the house and attended the funeral. I had to sit up front with the other pastors from around the village and the body was in a wooden box in front of us. After a couple of hours in that tent with the summer sun bearing down, the smell coming from the box and others wasn't pleasant, to say the least. From my seat, I could see outside the tent and the dirt road. One thing I noticed, or didn't notice, was the hearse that was supposed to come and take the body to the cemetery. As soon as the funeral was finished, I looked for my wife and told her we needed to go because I really didn't want to go to the cemetery and spend that time. As we were going to the truck, the pastor found us and wanted to talk. He said there was a problem, the hearse had not arrived. *Oh, really?* He said he had looked around the area and there were many cars but only one truck. Guess who, *by the divine appointment of God*, drove a truck to the funeral that day? *(Greedy nut!)*

The truck had a canopy with a door that opened like a normal door on the back. It wasn't very big, but big enough for them to slide the casket in the door with only about 2 feet sticking out the back and about a foot clearance at the top. The hole at the top was just big enough for them to push two men into the canopy to hold the casket in *since I forgot the rope.* They took Karen out of the truck and she rode with others and another pastor rode with me to lead the procession. When all the cars and buses were behind us, I asked my passenger where to go. He said since this was his first time there, he had no idea. So neither of us knew where the cemetery was located. I sat there until I saw my pastor's car pull out and come up beside us. He asked why we weren't moving. We told him. He said, "Follow me," and sped off down the dirt road. I had three women on each side of the "hearse" walking and singing. I asked the passenger what to do, and he said to speed up. I did and the women began walking faster. As we were getting left behind by the pastor, I asked my passenger again what to do. He said speed up a little more. I did and the women began jogging. Finally, it was either lose the lead car or stay with the jogging singers. I followed the car and left the women in the dust.

When we arrived at the cemetery, those same six women, although a little dusty, were standing there waiting, and still singing. Amazing! I pulled into the cemetery and they took the casket out and over to the open grave. I was closing the door and about to leave when a couple of the men came over and asked me to give them the spades (shovels). I asked, "What spades?" They replied, "The hearse driver always brings the spades to cover the grave." I thought, *"Great, do I really look like a hearse driver?"* I told them I'd see what I could do. I looked over and another group was just finishing covering their grave and sitting down to rest. I walked over and asked if we could borrow their spades. They said, "The hearse driver always brings the spades to cover the grave." *Really?* We borrowed theirs anyway. All was well. *(Nuts!)*

This is the Scripture I read later. I had learned a lesson that day.

"A man finds joy in giving an apt reply – and how good is a timely word! The path of life leads upward for the wise to keep him from going down to the grave. . . A greedy man brings trouble to his family, but he who hates bribes will live." Proverbs 15:23-24, 27.

African Culture

It was cool learning things about the different African cultures and then being able to tell our friends and family about these things. I was able to teach in a high school for one year which helped me understand more about the African youth culture. I taught the class, Biblical Studies, to all the 9th graders, all 450 of them in 6 classes. Yes, that is approximately 75 per classroom. We kept it as basic as I could make it, but did see some progress in several lives and met some great students and teachers in the process.

One cultural norm there is that when guys become close friends, they hold hands. Now, hear me on this. If that is your preference, that's your preference, I just don't happen to share that preference with you. It was really a weird feeling for me, after I became friends with several adult male youth leaders within the Baptist Convention that I worked with, for them to come up and take my hand and walk that way. On one hand (no pun intended), I wanted to let go, but on the other, I was glad that we had finally broken through some of those culture barriers and had become good friends.

I loved it when a good friend of mine, a single guy named Ken, from the USA, came for a visit. He went with Karen and me and some of our village youth on a mission trip to the north. After several days of working, we were having our nightly group devotion time, and one of the youth guys reached over and took Ken's hand and held it. I could see the expression on his face. Then, one of the guys on the other side did the same with Ken's other hand. I really had to try hard to keep from laughing out loud, because I knew the feeling he was experiencing right then. Afterwards, I explained about that cultural norm to him and he felt better about things.

(Nut! He was not impressed.)

Youth Camps

As we worked within the Baptist Convention of Southern Africa, we became good friends with several adult youth workers and their families. I would travel with these men to different parts of South Africa as we met with and did leadership training with other Convention groups.

There were three men in particular with whom I spent a lot of time. Peter (single at the time) was the Chairman of the Youth Convention, Elias (married to Elsie) was Secretary, and John (married to Elsie's sister, Sophia) was Treasurer. I remember during one particular leadership meeting we were having, there were many questions being asked and answered. As we were near the end of the meeting John walked in, late as usual, and sat in front of me. He started asking questions that we had already asked and answered. I would lean up to him, pat him on the shoulder, and tell him, "John, we've already talked about that, move on." He would ask another question and I would do the same thing again. After about four of those times, John stood up and said, "Mr. Chairman, Ron is abusing me from the floor." *Dude. What can I say? (Nut!)*

One weekend, the men and I traveled to a Youth Retreat, way out in a village somewhere. At the end of the Friday night meeting, a man took Peter and me to a family's home in the village. Behind the main home were several smaller huts that had been built, as kids were born, to be used as their bedrooms. The lady of the house took us to one of the huts and told us to have a nice night.

The hut consisted of a concrete floor, one double bed in the middle of the room, with two buckets of water and 2 towels for us to use to bathe. The tribal African culture says there is always room for one more. So in many of their homes, as many people as could sleep on a bed could be invited to sleep there. This is the case in many non-American cultures. It doesn't matter if you are a couple or several men or several women.

After we each did our thing with the buckets of water and towels, one on each side of the bed, I looked at Peter and said, "Peter, have you ever slept in the same bed with a white man?" Peter replied in the negative. So, I said, "Well, it's like this Peter. I'm married and I sleep with my wife. So, in the middle of the night, if I turn over and give you a hug, think nothing about it." Peter's eyes got big and he said, "Are you serious?" I said, "Oh, I'm very serious." It was really funny because Peter was a single man and this whole thing was a cultural oddity to him as well.

When we got into the bed, Peter laid down on one side of the bed and put his arm down along the side of the bed as if to hug the edge of the bed. I had him scared to death. So, I actually had a good night's rest because I had the whole rest of the bed to myself! I don't think either one of us moved the whole night. Peter never knew what to think about this *crazy American nut*.

I remember another Youth Retreat we were on where

we slept in school classrooms. The area hosts had brought in many single bed steel frames and mattresses, and had lined them up along the walls, with each bed pressed right up against the next one. That way, instead of just having 2 people sleep on 2 beds, you could get at least 3-4 on 2 beds. But, at the end of the line of beds, there was one that had about 3 feet of separation from the others. That was mine! Thanks guys!

Remember, a line in South Africa is called a "queue." At my first youth camp, when preparing to lead a game, I told the youth to form a line. They just stared at me and didn't move. I told them again and got the same response. I asked Peter if I was missing something. He asked, "What do you want them to do?" I said, "Stand one behind the other." He told me I wanted them to queue up. So, when I said, "Queue up!" they immediately lined up. *(Young nuts!)*

Also at that first camp, I knew beforehand to take my own eating utensils in addition to your bedding and personal toiletries. So, trying to fit into the culture, I went to the local hardware store and bought the camping plate, bowl, and cup, all made of metal. I learned something else at that camp, metal gets really hot when hot coffee or hot oatmeal are poured into it! So, after burning my hands at that first breakfast, I took a small towel with me the rest of the time to act as a pot holder for my metal dishes. When I got home we replaced the metal dishes with plastic! *(Smart nut!)*

When we were driving to that camp in my kombi,

those three men told me that the camp was in a certain town. So my goal was to drive to that town, thinking we had arrived. When we got to the town, they said to pull into a petrol station so they could get directions to the teacher's college where the camp was being held. Well, camp wasn't really at that town, it was at a location 30 miles away from town. That was when their "here" verses "just here" started to make sense.

Afrikaner People Group

When we lived in Bophuthatswana, we were the white family living in a black area. So, naturally, everyone we associated with was non-white. We learned a lot about their culture and history. And, since this was during the Apartheid era, there were a lot of stories talking about white against black, non-white against white, history. So, we learned their side of things.

The white race in South Africa that was pretty much tied up in the history of Apartheid were the Afrikaners. These folks would be defined as Afrikaans-speaking natives of South Africa of European, especially Dutch, descent. They were also referred to as Boers, descendants of any of the Dutch or Huguenot colonists who settled in South Africa, mainly in Cape Colony, the Orange Free State, and the Transvaal.

Since we lived in a non-white environment, we didn't have friends who were Afrikaners. In fact, we sort of looked on these folks as the enemy, as least that is how it seemed from what we had heard. That was until we moved to the Johannesburg area later on and met many great Afrikaans friends.

On one trip home from a Youth Camp down on the coast, we would encounter the Afrikaans culture in an upfront and personal way that would change our view of this people group forever.

Afrikaner Good Samaritans

Traveling the roads of South Africa during the 1990's was a bit rough and wild. There were no gas stations or rest areas along the national roads, we had to get off the main roads and go into small towns for gas and food and overnight accommodations. Towns could be very far apart, and traveling from one of the coasts to Johannesburg would mean kilometers and kilometers of desert and brush. People didn't normally stop to help motorists during those days with all the violence and crime.

On that trip home from Youth Camp, it was on one of those desolate stretches of roadway that our van pulling a trailer just quit. There was the Lomax family: mom, dad, and three kids, with one being a baby, stalled along the road with no town in sight and darkness was coming fast. What were we going to do?

We stood beside the road for a long time with darkness coming. We had no idea what to do, but prayed that someone would stop to help. Those were the days before cell phones and there was not an AAA service to call anyway. Many cars and vans passed and kept going. It was going to be very unsafe to spend a night along the road, but nowhere to go. If we didn't have our kids with us I would have felt better.

Finally, a car pulling a camper trailer passed and slowed down. They pulled off the road up ahead of us and turned around. They came and passed us by again going the other direction. I told Karen they had done that. They turned around again and this time came and pulled over just in front of our van. There was a dad, mom, and two children in the small car. And they were Afrikaners! We could tell by their accent when the man spoke to us in English.

After telling them our story, the man told us that it was going to be very unsafe to stay here, and we knew that. He told us there was a small town a few kilometers down the road, but didn't want to just take me and leave my family on the road. So, they loaded our family into their car, nine of us in the car. They drove us into the small town and it was dark by this time. He said he knew where the gas station/garage was located and would try that first.

Do any of you remember what went on at night in small towns, especially in the south where I grew up, before there were fancy electronic gadgets? Guys would gather around a garage and tinker with their cars. And that is exactly what was going on at the local garage! There were several men, backyard mechanics, gathered around a truck, and I'm not really sure what the issue was with the truck.

We stopped to see if they could offer some advice or help. Not one of them understood English. They all spoke Afrikaans. We didn't speak Afrikaans at the time, we would only learn that later when we moved to Cape Town. Well, it just so happened that we were with an Afrikaans family who spoke both Afrikaans and English!

So, they interpreted for us. One of the men owned the garage and he told us there was a man who owned a "break down" a few streets over. I had no idea what he was talking about. My interpreter told me that a "break down" was what I would call a "tow truck." I was thinking to myself, "I don't need a 'break down,' I'm already broke down, I need a tow truck!"

We drove over to that man's house and he agreed to help us get my van and trailer off the highway and into town. So, he and I went after the van and brought it to the garage while the Samaritan family stayed with my family in town, and continued to be our interpreters.

When we got the van to the garage, those mechanics tore into it right away to see if they could assess the damage. They almost immediately told me it was probably the crank shaft that was broken and would need to be replaced. Obviously, they would need to call a parts store in a larger town the next day to have the part delivered for repairs to be done. We needed to figure out what we would do for the night.

There was a small hotel in town but it was full, someone was having a family reunion. One of the Afrikaner young men at the garage told us, through our interpreter who was still with us, that he lived in the larger town many kilometers away, but his parents lived there in town, just a street over, and were away on vacation. He told us that we could stay at their house, he would go to the neighbor and get the key.

Since things seemed like they would be taken care of, our Good Samaritan Afrikaner family said goodbye and continued on their way. I got their details so we could communicate with them later. What a God-send and answered prayer!

So, this other young man whom we had obviously never met, unlocked his parent's house so we could have a place to stay for the night. He gave us the two bedrooms and he slept on the sofa in the living room. The next morning he went to the shop and brought back to the house some eggs, bread, bacon, and milk for our breakfast. He told me, in very broken English, to use what we wanted, he had to get back to the city for work. He said, "When you get ready to leave, give the key to the owner of the garage, he will get it back to the neighbor. If the van is not finished today, stay another night, my parents won't be home for another week, they won't mind." And, with that, he left.

The garage was able to get the part by noon and had the van repaired by around four o'clock in the afternoon, exactly 24 hours after our break down out on the highway the day before. What an answer to prayer! How God had taken care of us, using a group of people whom we had never had the chance to be around or get to know. We met some of the most generous Afrikaans people in that small South African town and have never forgotten their service and kindness to us, including the family who became our Good Samaritans.

Luke 10:25-37 *The Story of the Good Samaritan*

Stalking Lions

One of our missionaries, Ed, who directed a human needs relief project in the north was retiring and leaving the field. Since I lived closest to the project, I was asked to take over until we decided how long it would continue. The project took care of Mozambique refugees coming into South Africa, fleeing civil war in their country. These refugees would walk across the Kruger National Game Park to get into South Africa. There are huge electric lines running across the park and the refugees called this the Freedom Highway. They knew that if they could follow those lines, they would be lead to freedom. Since this game park is a place where the African animals live in the wild, South African game rangers would often find human remains left behind by animals.

One night I was at our base camp near Kruger Park and five young men came limping into camp. They were very tired and very hungry. As they were eating a meal, they told us about their journey across the park. A pride of lions followed them for four days so they couldn't stop to rest or sleep. They just kept walking. We found this story to be amazing because God protected them from the lions. Before going to bed, we shared with them the following verse about a loving God who protects His children.

"My God sent his angel, and he shut the mouths of the lions. They have not hurt me, because I was found innocent in his sight." Daniel 6:22.

God Heals the Sick

The Mozambique refugees lived in camps spread out across that northern area of South Africa. There were various numbers of people in different camps. We would help refugees find which camp they might have relatives in and get them to those camps. The International Mission Board's Human Needs Department provided food to feed those in many of these camps. We delivered food by truck to different camps every day, hitting each camp twice per month, feeding approximately 3,000 families per month. We would take the food in, and while there would have a worship and teaching time with the people and a time to take care of minor medical needs.

Ed, who I went in with in the beginning had been a pharmacist prior to becoming a missionary, so he knew many of the diseases present and what medicines to dispense for various things. I'm clueless in that area and get sick when I see blood. I pass out getting a blood test or an injection. But, one day, people came running up to us and said a man was sick and needed us to go to him. As we arrived, the man was having an epileptic seizure. The only thing we could do was to hold him down and pray for him. The people thought he was having a demonic attack because we were holding him down and praying over him. When the seizure abated and he sat up, and then, stood up, the people assumed we had healed him. We were able to help them understand that we serve a great God and He loves His people. We had no power in our hands, only God can heal where and when He deems it to happen.

"And the prayer offered in faith will make the sick person well; the Lord will raise him up. If he has sinned, he will be forgiven. Therefore confess your sins to each other and pray for each other so that you may be healed. The prayer of a righteous man is powerful and effective." James 5:15-16.

Another experience with a healing type ministry came one night when I took two other missionary men with me to a tent crusade in that northern part of South Africa. I usually didn't like to attend some of these tent crusades because they got a little weird based upon my beliefs. On that night the preacher preached a good, evangelistic sermon and gave a very clear invitation to those who wanted to accept Jesus Christ as their personal Savior.

I had just commented to the other men how good that was when the one who had preached gave the microphone to another preacher present. He proceeded to tell all who needed healing to come to the front. At that point, I told the men to follow me out of the tent. When we were about to leave the tent, I heard over the sound system that there were three Baptist missionaries present at tonight's service and they would now come to the front and pray over and heal those coming forward. *Aah, man, preacher nut!*

He had the people line up in three lines, one for each of us. Since all eyes were on us, we turned around and walked to the front. The preacher looked at me and handed me the microphone. I stood in front of the people and explained my position on healing. When I told them that my hands held no healing power whatsoever, you could hear the gasp across the tent. I told them we were going to lay our hands on them and pray for God to work in their hearts. I explained that we believed in and served a living God who loved them and wanted the best for them.

I have no problem in accepting the miraculous and in believing that miracles can happen at any moment in the will and sovereignty of God. But, that's when they happen, in the will and sovereignty of God. His plan. His choice. Not ours.

So, that night, we did lay our hands on those who had come forward. We prayed for each of them, that God would have His way in their hearts and lives. If it was according to His will, healing would come. Believing in faith, we continue to leave the results to our Lord.

"Jesus replied, 'What is impossible with man is possible with God.'" Luke 18:27.

"Now faith is confidence in what we hope for and assurance about what we do not see." Hebrews 11:1.

4 JOHANNESBURG – SOWETO

Thusong Baptist Centre *("Place of Help")*

To meet a growing need, our Mission decided to start a vocational training center outside the township of Soweto, Johannesburg. At that time, Soweto (which means South Western Townships), was the largest township in South Africa. There were thousands of people living in various sizes and makes of houses and thousands more living in squatter camps. Squatter camp residents were people who had moved into the city to find jobs, but the problem was they had no job skills. If they could learn some skills, they could go to work to take care of their families. The old saying of, "Give a man a fish, he eats for the day, teach a man to fish, he eats for a lifetime," is so true, and we saw that lived out among these people.

I became the Director of this vocational training center, so my family moved onto the Center property, a 50-acre farm in a "location" called Suurbekom ("place of sour water"). The Center's name was Thusong Baptist Center (Thusong meaning, "a place of help"). We taught vocational classes of welding, motor mechanics, masonry, auto body repair (they call it "panel beating"), sewing, typing, candle-making, and gardening. There were also 600 laying hens on the property. We sold eggs and used the droppings for fertilizer in the field and gardens.

There were even 15 hives of African killer bees on the property, which was the cause of some consternation every so often among the people. Our bus and truck driver, Chester, found out one day that the bees didn't like him running into their hives with the tractor while he was mowing with the bush hog! Seeing Chester run across the field with a dark cloud of bees following him was pretty funny to the rest of us. *(Nut!)* And, yes, he left the tractor in the field with the motor still running.

The class sessions would last anywhere from seven to ten weeks. We sent our bus into Soweto every morning to collect the students and took them home in the afternoon. There were 70-80 students per session. Every morning began with a devotion and the only rules were that everyone had to attend and sleeping wasn't allowed. Those of us working at the Center would take turns leading the devotions.

We had several African guys living and working there with us, plus another short-term missionary couple and other Americans here and there. We knew from the beginning that a seven-foot tall concrete panel wall would have to be built around the property because theft is a definite reality in South Africa. The wall stretched for two kilometers around the 50 acres. Later, after we discovered that chickens were being stolen at night, we had to add two feet of razor wire to the top of the wall. That took us two weeks and many pairs of leather gloves to install. There was also a steel electric gate across the driveway near the road, installed after the razor wire went up.

It seemed like each day brought something new to our experience of working with the guys at the Center. One day one of the workers, Zachariah, came into my office with a broken wrench. He said, "The wrench broke." I asked him if he broke it, to which he replied, "No, it just broke." I asked him if it broke while he was using it. He told me it did break while he was using it, but he didn't break it, it just broke.

There was a history of losing keys by all the workers, so I welded a large ring and attached the wad of keys to it. The ring was so large it wouldn't fit into their pockets, they had to carry the ring or wear the ring on their arm.

Each week, different workers were responsible for the key ring because it was their week to do particular chores that required the keys. On one of Zach's weeks, the keys got lost. I asked him if he lost them. The reply was, "No, they got lost." I asked him if he had been carrying them when they got lost, and again the reply was, "No, they just got lost." I asked him if perhaps he had put them down and forgot where he put them. The reply was, "No, I don't remember putting them down. They just got lost."

We retraced his steps for the day and did not find the ring of keys. So, once again, we had to replace all the keys and the ring. Several months later while one of our men was using the tractor and plow in the field, he uncovered the rusted ring of keys. Zach had evidently lost them while harvesting something in the field months earlier.

(Nut, Zach!)

Stolen at Gunpoint

One morning, Karen was getting ready to take our kids to school about 13 kilometers (8 miles) away. She had our three children in the van, and had opened the gate to collect 3 more African children for the ride to school. Two men with guns ran through the gate, put one gun to Karen's head and told her in an African language to get out of the van. She got out with all the children and they took the van, which we never saw again. That was the day we arranged for 24-hour armed guards on the property. Losing chickens and crops were one thing, lives were a different story. Remember our prayer for protection and peace?

Let your reasonableness be known to everyone. The Lord is at hand; do not be anxious about anything, but in everything by prayer and supplication with thanksgiving let your requests be made known to God. And the peace of God, which surpasses all understanding, will guard your hearts and your minds in Christ Jesus. Philippians 4:5-7

Notice the two areas of peaceful protection we can expect from our Heavenly Father: our hearts and our minds. God will guard those two parts of us, eighteen inches apart, which seem to plot against us. If our hearts are troubled, it won't be long before our minds will be as well. If our thoughts are headed in the wrong direction, our hearts will soon follow. But God's peace, the assurance of His control, can guard both heart and mind no matter what we are facing.

Right now, there are Christians experiencing God's

peace while going through unbelievable things. Their assurance in the face of evil and pain is a testimony that brings glory to God, for it is clear to those watching that something **which surpasses all understanding** is going on. These Christians are getting supernatural help! Like Shadrach, Meshach, and Abednego, they are in the furnace, but they are still walking around.

Almost 700 years before Paul wrote to the Philippians, Daniel's friends Shadrach, Meshach, and Abednego were living out this passage in the face of great opposition. They were rejoicing in the Lord always, letting their reasonableness be known to everyone, recognizing the Lord was at hand, and experiencing the peace that far surpassed King Nebuchadnezzar's understanding. That is, until he saw how God showed up *in the furnace*!

Think of those young Jewish men standing near a roaring furnace, knowing they were about to be fed to the flames *(see Daniel 3:8–30)*. They weren't sure they wouldn't die. Their peace came from being sure that no matter what happened, God would deliver them.

Peace is easy to understand when everything is going well, but not so easy when circumstances get hard. God's peace is always available, and He wants you to rest in it—especially in seasons of darkness and difficulty. The peace that **surpasses all understanding** is one of the best gifts God has to give!

Remember, you don't get to choose your furnaces.

But you can choose to live rejoicing in the Lord. You can choose to get along with others and practice anxiety-free days as you turn everything over to God with thanksgiving. Even if you don't fully understand *how* to go through challenges with a calm, quiet confidence, this will not prohibit God's ability to give you the gift of peace. And that peace is a powerful way to draw others to the God who has graciously given it.

"You are my hiding place; you will protect me from trouble and surround me with songs of deliverance." Psalms 32:7.

Well, continuing along the theft route – another time at the Center, our cook lady, Lizzie, came into my office and told me there were many tea spoons missing. A few days later, more spoons went missing. Then, the toilet roll holder disappeared from the students' restroom. Next, we lost the glass shelf over the toilet! Several days later, the large wooden/rubber spatula that is used in the silk-screening class was discovered to be missing.

I decided to get all the students from that particular class out on the driveway and told our workers to look through all their belongings. No one had a problem with that except for one small, older man wearing a trench coat! We told him to open his coat, which he didn't really want to do. When he did, the spatula fell out. There were several spoons in the pockets which he'd just lifted that day! Obviously, he wasn't invited to come back to school, he was expelled, the kleptomaniac nut.

Church Start

One day a group of students came into my office and wanted to talk. They said, "Moruti (Pastor), you know we have been here for many weeks. And, you know that we listen to the devotions every morning. And, you know some of us have accepted Jesus as our Lord and Savior. And, you know we don't have a church in our camp, so what are you going to do about it?" What a great question!

The next Sunday, which happened to be Easter Sunday, we took a contingent from Thusong and went out to their squatter camp and had a worship service in the small dirt-packed yard of one of their shacks. We went back every Sunday for three months and met in that yard, with more people joining us each week. We started a Sunday School class for the kids in a shack at another yard.

One Sunday the kids were in the shack, standing and singing. My wife was outside trying to figure out how to get the keys out of the ignition of our vehicle with the doors locked! One of the windows was down a little bit, so she sent our son into the shack to borrow a chair. Well, he did that, but he borrowed the chair which was directly behind an American missionary lady who was working with us at Thusong, along with her husband, for two years. And, no, he forgot to tell her he was borrowing her chair! After the song was over, everyone sat down. There was a very loud thud, indicating someone had fallen against the tin wall of the shack. Guess who that was?

After three months, the rainy season was about to start and the yard wouldn't be a good idea any longer. So, with help from our workers and the church people, we built a 10'x20' tin and pole building which became the Protea Baptist Church *(it was in the Protea squatter camp)*. We pitched a large tent outside in the church yard for some evangelistic services to take place over the next few weeks. After one week, someone stole that tent during the night and we never saw it again. It probably went to the same place as the van which we never saw again. *(Bad nuts!)*

But, people were saved by God's grace in that church. One Sunday, a lady came in late, and the people sitting near the front moved to let her sit on the front bench by herself. No one wanted to sit by her. When I questioned Chester about this later I was told she was the community witch doctor. She came back the next week, and the next week, and slowly the people started sitting with her and speaking to her. After several more weeks, the witch doctor gave her heart to the Lord and ended up burning her tools of the trade which provided her livelihood. Then, she had to get a real job to support herself, which she was able to do. She had put her trust in the Lord and He had provided for her needs.

We were able to have many baptismal services at Thusong in the swimming pool that was already there when the mission bought the farm. On one of these occasions, I was blessed to baptize my own son after his profession of faith and acceptance of Jesus Christ. Those were very good days with the church.

A great footnote here – years after we helped start that church, we were living down in Cape Town where we had moved on after Thusong. One of the young men from the church, Thabiso, who was there when we started, called me and asked if I would preach the anniversary sermon. When I asked him where he wanted me to preach, he said, "Well, at the Protea Baptist Church, where else? We are 10 years old!" Wow, how time had flown. We flew up to Johannesburg and had a great reunion with our friends at the church, which is still going strong and reaching people for the Lord Jesus Christ. And, when I last had contact with them, that same young man who helped us build the church had been to seminary and was now Pastor of the church. Great stuff!

Foolish Builder

There were many funny stories that happened at Thusong with the men who lived with us on the farm. The men who worked for us could live on the property but they had to abide by the rules. A couple of the rules were that they couldn't bring girls onto the property after hours and they had to be home before the gate was locked and the dogs were let out to patrol at around 11:00 p.m.

One worker, Bennett, didn't like these rules and said he wanted to move to the squatter camp. He asked if he could have some old tin he found lying around the Center. I told him he could move and have the material, but he wouldn't find anywhere to build, all the sites were taken. He didn't like that answer and told me he would find a place for his shack.

A few days later, Bennett came to me and was so proud. He told me about finding a place with grass where no one else was smart enough to build and he had the place to himself. I couldn't quite understand where that might be because the squatter camps had mostly hard-packed dirt with very little grass.

The next Sunday when we went out for church, I walked over to see Bennett's shack. He had built one of the ugliest shacks I had ever seen right in the middle of a dry river bed. It was the dry season, but guess what? There is a reason why that river bed runs through that area and, as Bennett stated, no one else was *smart enough* to build there! When I pointed this out to him he got mad and said I just didn't want him to be happy with his own place. So, I gave him my blessing, such as it was, and left it at that.

Well, about three weeks later, the rains started. That first night I remember how hard it rained and how much fell in a short amount of time. The next day when Chester came in with the busload of students, guess who stepped off the bus, soaked, carrying everything he had left, which was one shoe, a plastic bag of clothes, and a waterlogged blanket! Yep, Bennett.

"So, Bennett, should I ask what happened to you?"
"Moruti *(Pastor)*, you wouldn't believe it. In the middle of the night, something hit my shack, and when I woke up, my mattress was floating. The door was open and my stuff was floating out the door and down the river. I lost everything except these things." *(At that point, I thought, "What was he going to do with one shoe?").* He continued, "I just got to high ground when my whole shack broke and went down the river. Can I come home?"
"Yes, Bennett, but you know we have rules here."
Bennett answered, "No problem!" *(Nutcase!)*

That experience with Bennett brought new meaning to two different Bible stories; one, of the foolish builder, and the other, the story of the prodigal son. He decided it would be better to live at Thusong with rules than on a float trip down the river.

"Therefore everyone who hears these words of mine and puts them into practice is like a wise man who built his house on the rock. The rain came down, the streams rose, and the winds

blew and beat against that house; yet it did not fall, because it had its foundation on the rock. But everyone who hears these words of mine and does not put them into practice is like a foolish man who built his house on sand. The rain came down, the streams rose, and the winds blew and beat against that house, and it fell with a great crash." Matthew 7:24-27

Luke 15:11-32 – Story of the Prodigal Son
"The son said to him, 'Father, I have sinned against heaven and against you. I am no longer worthy to be called your son.'
"But the father said to his servants, 'Quick! Bring the best robe and put it on him. Put a ring on his finger and sandals on his feet. Bring the fattened calf and kill it. Let's have a feast and celebrate. For this son of mine was dead and is alive again; he was lost and is found.' So they began to celebrate." vv. 21-24

Soup Kitchen

When we would have many students from one particular squatter camp learning skills, we would try to help them with food or meals for families until they could go to work and earn their own way. One instance of this was a soup kitchen we did at the Mandela Squatter Camp in Soweto. I will never forget our first day there, definitely not one of the safest places in Soweto.

Zachariah, and I were in the small truck and Chester was driving the 4-ton truck with the cast iron pots, wood for the fire, and soup powder. Zach and I drove up to the front of a community center and parked. We got out to walk around to the back of the center where Chester was coming with the supplies. When we rounded a back corner of the building, there were 12-15 young men running at us with guns and machete-like knives. We wondered, "What do we do now? There is nowhere to run!"

We stopped in our tracks and Chester saw what was taking place so he stopped the truck beside us and hopped out to stand with us. When the young men got pretty close to us, they stopped and probably saw that we didn't know what was happening. I'm not sure if it was the look on my face or on Zachariah's, but it was one of those moments when you really didn't have time to think because it happened so fast. One of the men said to us, "Wait, you don't understand, we're here to protect you while you feed our people." He went on to tell us there dangerous people around there so they would stay with us. *Dude. What a relief. (Scary Nuts!)*

I told them that I thought they could protect us without the guns, just with their presence. After they asked if I was sure, they collected all the weapons and took them to a hiding place. We were protected that day as always. Thank you, Lord. After the little run-in with the gun-wielding men, Zach told me he was so scared that he thought he had prayed his last prayer. I told him he did well by just thinking to pray.

When Jesus prayed for His disciples prior to His arrest, He prayed, *"I will remain in the world no longer, but they are still in the world, and I am coming to you. Holy Father, protect them by the power of your name – so that they may be one as we are one. . . My prayer is not that you take them out of the world but that you protect them from the evil one." "My prayer is not for them alone. I pray also for those who will believe in me through their message, that all of them may be one, Father, just as you are in me and I am in you. May they also be in us so that the world may believe that you have sent me."*
John 17:11, 15, 20-21.

Waiting for the Darkness

A prayer for protection and good health was a constant prayer of ours for our family throughout our career in South Africa. Many people take these things for granted, but we didn't because we had lived through situations where God honored that prayer on a regular basis. We continue to thank God for these things.

One weekend, Nut Magnet #1 and I were helping lead a youth conference in a place called Hammanskraal. Fighting between the people and the government was still taking place so one never knew what would happen next. We went to bed on Friday night knowing there was a lot of unrest in the area, as well as a lot of racial hatred and fighting rearing up around the country. People were being killed on all sides.

We got up on the Saturday morning and saw one particular story in the newspaper, with pictures, where three white Afrikaans men had been brutally murdered in the mix of all that was taking place in Bophuthatswana and South Africa as a whole. *(These men who were shot had helped incite the trouble but that doesn't necessitate murder.)* Our colleagues at the retreat came to us and showed us the front page of the newspaper with the photo of the murdered men. We prayed about the situation. They told us that we needed to leave that area and drive back to Johannesburg, to Thusong. Some of them would go with us, but we couldn't leave during the daylight because it wasn't a good thing to have a person of white skin driving on the roads in that area at that time. So, we waited until darkness fell, and then left to make the drive home, which we did without further incident. I had called my wife in Johannesburg and told her we were coming so please have supper and mattresses ready for ten more folks! Thankfully, because of the 600 laying hens on the property, there were plenty of eggs.

His Loving Presence
"When you go through deep waters, I will be with you. When you go through rivers of difficulty, you will not drown. When you walk through the fire of oppression, you will not be burned up; the flames will not consume you. For I am the Lord, your God, the Holy One of Israel, your Savior." Isaiah 43:2-3

Have you ever felt as though everyone has let you down? Have you ever felt abandoned or forgotten or forsaken?

Paul the apostle felt that way. Imprisoned at Jerusalem, Paul must have been feeling discouraged, because we read in Acts 23:11, *"The following night the Lord stood by him and said, 'Be of good cheer, Paul.'"*
God reminded him that he was not alone.

In one of his books, the great British preacher C. H. Spurgeon said:

> If all else forsook him, Jesus was company enough; if all despised him, Jesus' smile was patronage enough; if the good cause seemed in danger, in the presence of His Master, victory was sure. The Lord who had stood *for* him at the cross, now stood *by* him in prison. . . . It

was a dungeon, but the Lord was there; it was dark, but the glory of the Lord lit it up with heaven's own splendor.

It comes down to this: I would rather be in a jail or in a storm or in a hardship with Jesus than anywhere else without Him. But the thing is, He is with us wherever we go. That is what the Lord was saying to Paul: "You are not alone."

Remember again what God says, *"When you go through deep waters, I will be with you. When you go through rivers of difficulty, you will not drown. . . . For I am the Lord, your God, the Holy One of Israel, your Savior."* Isaiah 43:2-3

Democracy Comes to South Africa

There was much concern in South Africa leading up to the first democratic election in 1994. Nelson Mandela had been released from prison and the two largest African tribal political parties were vying for position so their man could become President. In the end, the African National Congress (ANC) won the election and their man, Mandela, became the President of the country. What a President he would be.

Mandela was a very wise, patient, and humble man who became one of the greatest leaders the country has ever had. He was the right man for the job of bringing a divided country together for good. Don't get me wrong, South Africa had her problems during those days and since then. But, that time in the life of the country could have turned out so differently had Mandela not taken the reigns.

We would see a lot of change in the country over the next several years, having lived there during some of the Apartheid era and then into a time of democracy and transition.

Missionary Nuts

In the midst of all that was taking place in South Africa during those ending years of Apartheid and the new democratic elections to take place, we still found time to explore the beauty of the country and its people. I remember taking three and five-day backpacking hikes with fellow missionaries. Several of these hikes took place around the Blyde River Canyon in what was then the eastern Transvaal.

Two of the more memorable hikes took place on the five-day Otter Trail hike. This hike takes one from one bay to another five days later. A person hikes on the beaches of the Indian Ocean, high up on the cliffs, back through the valleys, and across the mouths of several rivers.

One such river needed to be crossed at low-tide due to the depth and current of the river at high-tide. Hikers have to be aware of the time for that day's low-tide, and even then, backpacks must be put in watertight bags and floated across the river to the other side. The day we crossed that river we had to leave the hut at 4:00 a.m. in order to reach the river at low-tide.

We had to carry everything we needed for five days, spending each night at huts along the way that had bunk beds and a three-inch foam mattress. We took our water out of rain barrels and had to filter out the mosquito larvae and boil it before use. But, what a relaxing evening was spent around the campfire after a great meal cooked on the fire and hearing stories about all kinds of things. I had some great missionary men to bond with during those times and we just shared life together. Let me tell you some things about these men, but nothing confidential of course! Some things said around the campfire stay at the campfire.

There was "Nut Magnet #1" with his great stories, and then there was me, "Nut Magnet #2." There was the guy who, as we were talking around the fire one night, told us about a job he had while he was in seminary, working as Goofy at Disneyland. This guy is about 6'5" tall, so at one point when he told us they had to extend the length on the costume, he blurts out that he was "probably the biggest Goofy in the world." Do you think we ever let him forget that blurb? No way. *(Nut #3)*

Then, there was the guy we all accused of having OCD *(obsessive compulsive disorder)*, whether that is a fair assessment or not. He is a friend and a great guy, otherwise I wouldn't talk about him! I'll refer to him as B.

When Nut Magnet #1 and I walked into our dorm room at Missionary Kid's Camp one day where several of us were counselors, B had his colored underwear folded and stacked on an empty bed in two piles. We assumed one was clean and one was dirty, but I don't guess a person could tell because they were all neatly folded and stacked. Well, Nut Magnet #1 asked if I thought this guy could tell if we altered the piles. So, he moved some pairs from one stack to the other, and vice versa. We were both lying on our respective bunks when B came into the room. He immediately looked at his underwear and said, "Okay, who's been messing with my underwear?" *How did he know?* He said, "What did you do, mix them up?" And, then went on, "Great, now I'm going to have to do the sniff test!" *Are you serious? I'm out of here. (Nut #4!)*

Nut Magnet #1, B, and I traveled together on several occasions during our sports evangelism days. On one of these occasions while at a basketball tournament, we were getting ready to leave our bed and breakfast place, and waiting for B to finish getting ready. Nut Magnet #1 came out of the bathroom and said B was just finishing up his 3rd shave of the morning. *Who shaves three times every morning?* He lathers up and goes up only, washes all that off, then does it all again, down only. He washes all that off and does it all again, this time side to side, just to make sure all is covered.

I must admit though that all that time spent around B made some of the others of us better organized men. I did start organizing my closet better which takes less time trying to see what goes with what. And to know which pair of tennis shoes goes with which track suit, surely that will come in handy.

B was also our electronics expert. He was our "go-to" guy for helping others of us out who were not electronic savvy. Nut Magnet #1 couldn't even use a computer until B taught him what he needed to know! I would always let B get the latest cell phone and learn all about it before I would buy the same phone and learn from him what I needed to know.

One thing about B and his cell phone, he would rarely turn it off or put it on vibrate. Sometimes we would get irritated when his cell phone went off in the middle of something. One night, B was speaking to a Youth Rally of approximately 200 young people. He was on the stage speaking with a microphone in one hand, his Bible and notes in the other hand, and his cell phone on his hip. I was sitting in the balcony with a few of the other youth leaders. I asked Marlon if he thought B's cell phone was on vibrate. He said he didn't believe it would be. So, we had to check it out! I called B's number, and sure enough, it began ringing on stage. The sight of B trying to figure out how to get the mic and his Bible into one hand while trying to silence the cell phone with the other hand, in front of all those youth who were laughing at him, was pretty funny.

On the way home, B jokingly said, "I'm going to kill my wife! She knows not to call me when she knows I'm in the middle of something." I just looked at him and started laughing. He said, "My wife didn't make that call, did she?" I replied, "No, that was Marlon and me in the balcony!" We had a good laugh on the way home, but he did start putting his phone on vibrate more often after that.

I wish you could hear Nut Magnet #1's stories. At one point or another throughout his life, he has been a missionary kid raised in Africa, soccer player, rugby player, baboon fighter, college football kicker *(the Swahili Sidewinder)*, pro football kicker, bodyguard, associate pastor, preacher, missionary, and just a great guy and a great friend to many, including me. Many of my stories have this guy as a player, since we seemed to manage to get into trouble together as easily as we could do it by ourselves. He was also the one who was with me on that retreat in Hammanskraal, when we had to leave under darkness.

He tells a story about a baboon named One-Eyed Jack. He was on his senior trip in Africa, he had graduated from a high school academy there. They were up in the treetops on a platform watching the animals at a waterhole. He said he was looking through the lens of a pair of binoculars and all of a sudden, blackness filled the screen. He looked up and One-Eyed Jack was eyeing his new pen his dad had given him for graduation.

The baboon had gotten his name for his one good eye, the other didn't work due to a beating he had gotten some time earlier because of his thievery. The baboon grabbed my friend's pen and ran to the other side of the platform. My friend was mad that the baboon had stolen his pen and told the game ranger about it. The ranger told him not to look at the baboon, he would retrieve the pen. The ranger went over to the baboon and told him to give him the pen. After a couple of minutes, the baboon gave him the pen. The ranger came across to my friend and told him to put the pen away and, whatever he does, don't look at One-Eyed Jack.

Well, you can probably guess what happened next, he had to look just once. When he did, One-Eyed Jack got really mad and attacked him, grabbing him around the leg and trying to bite through his jeans. My friend said he was screaming to get that baboon off him and the ranger was beating the baboon with his stick to get him off. Finally, he ran away and so did my friend, off the platform, not to return, but with his nice, new pen back in his pocket.

(One-eyed hairy Nut!)

Otter Trail Hostel

After a tough Otter Trail hike the second time, we spent the last night in a backpacker's hostel-kind-of-place on the bay. There must have been about 15 people, male and female, sleeping in that large upper room with one bathroom at the end of the room, our end.

One of my buddies was sleeping in the bed directly across from the bathroom door and I was beside him in another bed. In the middle of the night, I heard something, and woke up to see a girl standing at the foot of this guy's bed, shaking his foot to wake him up. He woke up and looked down at her standing there. The light was on in the bathroom. He asked her what she wanted. She was pointing at the bathroom floor and said, "There is a bug in the bathroom, what is it?" This guy looked over and said, "It's a scorpion." She asked if it was dangerous. He replied, "Deadly!" She wanted to know what to do. He told her to take his boot and kill it. So, a few seconds later, the whole room was awakened by this girl beating the scorpion to death with the boot against the wooden floor. The next morning, there was a squashed and very dead scorpion on the bathroom floor.

Kruger National Park

Many camping trips were taken during our earlier years in South Africa in the Kruger National Game Park. We love the African animals and being able to see them in their natural habitat. There are camps inside the park that have huge wooden fences with electric wire around them to keep the animals out. The gates close at dusk and open after sunrise. Most of our family from the USA who came to visit have witnessed and enjoyed Kruger National Game Park.

One trip we were camping in our trailer and a tent, and we had a new college graduate, a Journeyman, who had just gotten into the country. He was going to work with us for two years. He, another man missionary, and I were sleeping in the tent on the first night. Around 3:00 a.m. there was a sound on the other side of the fence and this college boy came straight up out of his sleeping bag. I asked what was wrong. He said, "Was that what I think it was?" I asked, "What do you think it was?" He replied, "Sounds like it could be a lion." "That's exactly what it is, a whole pride, now go back to sleep." He didn't.

We have seen magnificent animals in Kruger. The elephants amazed me more than any other animal, which probably explains the amount of elephants in our house today. It's a strange feeling to have your van parked on the road so a herd of elephants can cross the road on their way down to the river. Then to have an elephant charge your van because she thinks you are another animal threatening her baby, is a little unnerving. It's also very difficult to back a trailer in a hurry to turn around and drive the opposite direction. On one occasion when an elephant was charging us, my mother-in-law yelled at my father-in-law, who was videoing the scene out the passenger window, to close the window and lock the door, as if that would keep the charging elephant out of the van.

It seemed that we always had baboons climbing all over our van, which would scare our son to the point of hating every monkey he's ever come into contact with since! It didn't help that he was offering a baboon some popcorn through a hole in a cage one day and the baboon grabbed his hand and wanted to pull him into the cage. He was backpedaling that day. He didn't think it was as funny as the rest of us did.

One evening in Kruger, all of us except my wife and a daughter went on a late afternoon game drive. They stayed back at the camp to buy some eggs and get supper started. When we returned, my daughter replayed the scene of my wife fighting the monkey who tried to steal our eggs, an apparent tug-of-war had ensued with Karen winning. We had scrambled eggs that night!

(Nut monkey, what was he thinking?)

Furloughs

After three to five years on the mission field, missionaries were allowed a time back in the USA for furlough, or *stateside assignment* as it is called today. We enjoyed those times visiting with family and friends that we hadn't seen in some time. It was also a good time for our kids to meet some relatives they didn't even know since we lived so far away and couldn't attend all the family reunions and holiday times.

I remember one furlough when we were at a family Christmas party, one of our girls came over to us and asked if we loved these people. They weren't sure these people were like us! Our kids grew up speaking South African English, more similar to British English than American English. These relatives didn't speak English according to our kids.

School was very different for our kids on furlough. South African schools were very disciplined. Everyone wore a uniform, hair was kept short for boys or pulled back for girls, so there wasn't that peer pressure on clothing styles.

One day, one of our girls came home very upset. In class that day they had studied the American money system and how to count money. She said the teacher asked how many cents were in a quarter. Well, in South Africa, the time was either a quarter till or a quarter after, which would mean 15 minutes till or 15 minutes after the hour. So, when my daughter told the teacher a quarter was 15 cents, it was the wrong answer. That didn't make sense. When my daughter would go to a ballgame or a store where she had to pay with American money, she would put the money in her hand, hold out her hand and tell them to take what they needed.

When we traveled around to speak in churches, our whole family would be dressed in African clothing, often something tie-dyed! In the early days, we would get our kids to sing the South African national anthem. When they would all three sing, it was pretty good, but if our older daughter decided she didn't want to sing, it threw off the melody a bit.

I attended an associational mission celebration one week. During the week, at various events, I noticed that one missionary had a fantastic singing voice. I learned that music was his thing and was what he had been trained in. He was using those gifts as a missionary on the field. During the closing worship service, I stood in the row just in front of this missionary. After the service a lady in front of me turned around and told me that I had the most beautiful singing voice she had ever heard. I just acted humble and thanked her and walked away. Actually, that's not true. I had to tell her that she was actually hearing the voice behind me because I wasn't singing, I was listening to him!
(Nut, what was I thinking?)

During another week at an associational mission conference in North Carolina, Karen and I were to go out to a rural church and speak one night. Giving us directions, the Director of Missions told us to go out a certain road and when we got to the sign which read: "Welcome to Tennessee!" to turn around and take the first road on the right.

Well, that guy didn't know my superb sense of direction, I can usually find what I'm looking for, and this was before GPS in the car. So, I told Karen we are just going to take the last road on the left instead of going all the way to Tennessee, how hard can this be? So, we were driving down the road looking for that last road to the left when all of a sudden there was a huge sign that read: "Welcome to Tennessee!" We turned around and took the first road on the right.

Finally, I must tell you about the guy who accused me of being a stalker! Of all places, my wife and I and her parents were shopping in Penny's. While my wife and her parents were in one department, I decided to go to the men's department and look around. I noticed another man and a young girl in the store. The guy was large and looked a little unusual and we'll just leave it at that. We *were* in Poplar Bluff, Missouri, after all! *Poplar Bluff folks will get me for that one.*

As I walked into the men's department, I noticed this man looking at a tennis shoe that was on the sale rack. He moved on and I walked over and picked up that same shoe. I heard a voice say, "I was looking at that." I turned around and that man was staring at me. I held it up and asked, "This shoe?" He said, "Yeah, I was looking at that." I replied, "So, do you want it? You can have it. I bet they have more." He just walked off.

I kept looking around the men's department, and

every once in a while, there was that man again. It's not a large men's department. He finally weirded me out *("made me uncomfortable")* so I left that department and walked over to the jewelry display where a lady was working behind the glass counter.

Wouldn't you know it, here comes that nut, walking down the aisle toward the jewelry department. As I stepped up to the glass counter, the man yelled out toward the lady worker, "That man is stalking me!" We both looked at him in shock. I was dumbfounded to say the least. I had never been accused of stalking, especially from a weirdo man.

I looked at him and asked, "Are you talking about me?" He replied, "Yeah, you've been stalking me and I want it to stop!" I couldn't believe what I was hearing. What an idiot! I said, "I'm not sure what you're smoking, but I think you need to move along." I looked at the clerk and told her she might want to call the manager because this guy was a complete nut. She did.

The man got quiet and started looking at some other display. The manager came out and I asked him if he knew that man. He looked over at him and said he had never seen him before. I told him he might want to keep an eye on him because he was a nutcase. When we looked back around for the man, he and the girl were gone, vanished. What a strange experience. I found Karen and told her we needed to get out of there, there were some strange people in that place. Well, of course there were. There was a county seat super Wal-Mart next door! *(Super nut cases!)*

5 BEAUTIFUL CAPE TOWN

We lived in Cape Town the last 10 years we were in South Africa. The southern Cape has to be one of the most beautiful places on earth. In the Cape, added to the wildlife experience were the Southern Right whales that come into the bays every year. Unfortunately for our son, there are also many baboons in the Cape.

This is where our kids call home and where they spent the majority of their school years, with our two oldest graduating from high school there. We still miss our friends we have there and cherish those relationships.

Seminary Days

I had the opportunity to do many things in Cape Town through my various ministry work assignments. A few of those were: Associational Youth Worker, Baptist Seminary Youth Ministry Lecturer, Sports Evangelist, and Basketball Coach and Referee.

At the beginning of my first year at the Seminary, we went on the weekend retreat that starts off every new school year, to give the students, faculty, and families' time to get to know one another. There are four different year classes at the seminary, and one of the most anticipated events at the retreat is the annual "football" match between classes. Remember, their "football" is our "soccer." The students get to invite faculty onto their teams, so the First Year class asked me to play "football" with them, so I did. I am not a "soccer" player and didn't know the terminology. I do know "football" and its terminology. Here were the instructions I was given. "You stand here in the middle of the pitch and tackle anyone who comes through." Simple enough for a "football" player.

I was at my position when the first player from the other team came through, "dribbling" the ball. I went after him and "tackled" him as they told me to do. He looked up at me from lying on the ground and shouted, "Ron, what are you doing?" I told him they told me to tackle anyone who came through, so that's what I did. Only then did they enlighten me on the meaning of "tackle" in "soccer!" I was actually just supposed to get the ball away from him with my feet. What kind of game is that, can't use your hands?

(Nutty game!)

When we had our first "get-to-know-each-other" student and faculty time, I was asked to share my story because I was the new lecturer on the block. All the students were sitting at the desks in front of me and all the "doctors" were sitting in chairs along the wall. One of the students asked me what they were to call me, what prefix went before my name? Now, you need to understand the title thing in South Africa, and especially among the school lecturers, administration, some pastors, etc. They enjoy their titles, I guess because of how long some of them work for them. I'm not one of those, so I decided to have some fun at the lecturers' expense. I told the students that they call one who has a Doctorate degree, Dr. Roy or Dr. Venter. So, keep doing that of course. However, my degree is a Master's degree, so I told them if they didn't want to just call me by my first name to call me Master Lomax. Dr. Roy quickly got my attention and said I could just call him Kevin. *(Nut, he was not going to call me Master!)*

Through teaching at the Seminary, it was really cool to work with so many great youth ministry leaders and be able to teach them a little while they taught me so much more. I loved our mission weeks where we would travel to a different part of the area or country and be involved in missions of some type. One year we traveled to Mossell Bay and were involved in a youth ministry effort which including conducting some type of "Come and See" event in the afternoons, and an evangelistic crusade at night. This is what we had been studying at the Seminary that semester, so we were trying it out in reality. One afternoon, our "Come and See" event was a basketball clinic on a parking lot of a bottle store (liquor store). That was the only paved, level place in the area and they give us permission to use their lot. Can anything good come from this? Oh yeah!

While the basketball clinic was going on, I noticed one girl in particular who was just standing on the side watching what was taking place. We tried to get her involved in the games but she wasn't interested. I don't think she was sure about us yet. Her name was Christy. No matter how hard our folks tried to involve her, she wasn't interested, but she watched. During a break in the action, we announced to all who were gathered there that our team would be down at the Baptist Church that night for a youth service, and they were invited to "come and see" what was going on.

That night, there was a great attendance at the church, almost everyone we saw at the basketball event was there, and guess what, even Christy was there with a few of her friends. The worship was great and glorifying to the Lord. His Name was lifted up. The speaker for the night did a great job of presenting the Gospel of Jesus to those in attendance. At the end of the service, he called for anyone who wanted to speak to or pray with someone about accepting Christ as Lord and Savior to come forward. Many of those young people came forward and went with counselors into classrooms to talk and pray. My friend, Nut Magnet #1, was there that night and he was one of the counselors who had gone in to pray with some of the youth. When he came out, he was happy that some of the young people had accepted Christ and were beginning their walk with Him. I asked him if he remembered any of their names. He hadn't been able to find a piece of paper so he had written their names on his hand, and when I looked at the names, guess who I saw? Yeah, Christy! She had just come to watch that afternoon and later came to know the Lord Jesus as a personal Lord and Savior. What a thrill for us to be part of that!

"For God so loved the world that he gave his one and only Son, that whoever believes in him shall not perish but have eternal life. For God did not send his Son into the world to condemn the world, but to save the world through him." John 3:16-17.

"Thomas said to him, 'Lord, we don't know where you are going, so how can we know the way?' Jesus answered, 'I am the way and the truth and the life. No one comes to the Father except through me.'"
John 14:5-6.

Sad Times

With the great times in Cape Town, there were also sad times. We had good missionaries in Cape Town with us. One couple had transferred from another part of Africa, and he was one of the lecturer's at the Seminary. He loved to walk and hike and to exercise. I once climbed Table Mountain with him and another local pastor, took us two hours to climb to the top with our backpacks containing our lunches. On top of the mountain, we ate our lunches and were getting ready to take the cable car down, so I leaned down to pick up this guy's backpack for him. It was still heavy. I asked what he had in there and he said rocks. I climbed for two hours with only a lunch in my pack and I thought that was heavy. This guy, a little older than me, climbed with his lunch and rocks in his pack because he wanted to be fit. (Nut, or not?)

This guy also loved to play tennis. Every week he and I and usually one or two more missionary friends from other organizations would play tennis. One day we were warming up and this guy had hit a ball to me and then he just stood there like he was thinking about something. I asked him if there was anything wrong and he said yes. Then, he just lay down on the court. We got to him and one of the other guys and I started doing CPR while the fourth guy ran inside the office to call the ambulance. The EMS folks came and took him to the hospital and pronounced him dead there. What a shock.

This was the guy we felt was one of the healthier

among us. But, we never know what the plan of God holds. All our days are numbered and only God knows when He will take us home to be with Him. There is one fact of life I know to be true, every one of us will die and then face judgment. It's our choice as to whether we want to spend eternity in Heaven or Hell. I choose life. I choose Jesus. I choose Heaven! Have you made that choice yet? God offers us the free gift of salvation, Jesus, His Son, our Savior.

"For the wages of sin is death, but the gift of God is eternal life through Jesus Christ our Lord."
Romans 6:23

"For it is by grace you have been saved, through faith – and this not from yourselves, it is the gift of God – not by works, so that no one can boast." Ephesians 2:8-9

Sports Evangelism

As I worked within youth ministry, I found myself doing more and more with sports ministry. Eventually that led to going full-time into sports evangelism ministry. I was coaching basketball at my son's high school and then organized our own basketball club and sports organization in South Africa. We were called International Sports Federation South Africa (ISFSA). That was our platform to use while working in many different areas and among several different religious groups in Cape Town. We were able to go into schools and other areas and coach basketball clinics while sharing our faith in Christ at the same time. It's easy to get friendship relationships started through sports, and then use those relationships to share Christ with others.

There was a basketball association in Cape Town where club teams and university teams competed against one another in various leagues. There were both youth and adult leagues, both women and men. In order for a team to compete in an upper league, it had to win the championship in a lower league and move up. The last place team in each league would go down one league the next year.

Our club began with a men's team in the bottom league, the Men's Second League. We won that league so moved up to the Men's First League the next year. At the same time, we started another men's team and entered it in the Second League. That year, both of our men's teams won their leagues, so the first team moved up to the Super League and the second team moved up to the Men's First League. Then, we started another men's team in the Second League, giving us three men's teams in our club. We also started a ladies' team the same way, they won their Second League the first year, so moved up to the Women's First League and we started another team in the Second League. This gave us two ladies' teams for the club. We then worked at building a Boys' Team and a Girls' Team which competed in the Youth League on Saturdays.

Our goal for the club was for Christian players to be able to play beside non-Christian players, using that opportunity to share their faith with others. We would have devotionals and prayer at practices and always began and ended our games with prayer. We had fun together and met a lot of people through the process.

Every year, ISFSA would sponsor a weekend basketball tournament and invite the best teams in the Cape Town League to take part. We would play games on Friday night and all day Saturday, with an Awards Banquet that evening. The teams looked forward to the ISF Shootout every year because as part of the tournament, we would invite a men's and ladies' team from the USA to come play. A Christian sports organization in the USA would send quality teams over and help us as we hosted and ran the tournament, but more importantly, as we shared Christ through playing basketball. The USA teams would normally have the upper hand and talent and win the tournament but occasionally one of our local teams would come out on top. Either way, we all enjoyed the weekend and especially the banquet at the end. We would invite all the participating teams and the technical team (scorekeepers, timekeepers, and referees) to enjoy a nice meal and awards time together. One of our USA team members or coach would be the featured speaker for the banquet and would share basketball-related stories and then his/her testimony and the plan of salvation. There would normally be another player or two who would also share personal testimony of the difference Christ has made in their lives and how He helps them live each day.

After one of these banquets, the head referee and his wife came up to us and were asking questions about our faith and salvation, about what they had heard during the banquet. The wife's comment was, "We've tried all the other religions, so we thought we would talk with you about yours." We talked with them and arranged for them to come over to our house for dinner and more talk. They came over and we could tell that the wife was more interested in talking about spiritual things than her husband. We arranged for Karen and this lady to attend an Alpha seeker class to take place at our church, which they did. It was during this class interaction that this lady accepted Jesus as personal Lord and Savior and started going to another Baptist church nearer their home. There were other players from a few of the teams who asked good questions, and some of them accepted the Lord. There were some Christians on a few of the teams who decided, after seeing the American teams play, that they would take a stronger stand for the Lord through their sport.

Basketball was a way to meet people and use the gifts and abilities God had given to us. All of us who worked through ISFSA had felt God's call on our lives to do that. What are you doing with God's call to you?

Just Do It
"In Joppa there was a disciple named Tabitha (in Greek her name is Dorcas); she was always doing good and helping the poor." Acts 9:36

One of the first things we seem to learn in life is to make excuses for not doing what we should. It reminds me of the three people the Lord talked about in Luke 14:16-20.

"A certain man was preparing a great banquet and invited many guests. At the time of the banquet he sent his servant to tell those who had been invited, 'Come, for everything is now ready.' But they all alike began to make excuses. The first said, 'I have just bought a field, and I must go and see it. Please excuse me.' Another said, 'I have just bought five yoke of oxen, and I'm on my way to try them out. Please excuse me.' Still another said, 'I just got married, so I can't come.'"

One lame excuse after another. What good farmer would buy land he had not seen? Who would test oxen after buying them instead of before?

It's so easy to get sidetracked with other things and never finish what we set out to do. And whenever we talk about it, we can usually come up with a new excuse why we haven't done it yet. The truth here is, when God issues the invitation, there is no good excuse for refusing to accept. Whatever God is calling you to do, just do it!

Journeymen

A highlight of working as a missionary overseas was the camaraderie of working with other missionaries, both within our organization and with missionaries from other Christian mission organizations. Within our organization, there were several different ways to serve as a missionary. One of these was career missions, which is what we were, but another way was through the Journeyman and International Service Corps programs where folks could go and work for a limited time, most time periods being two years. We enjoyed having several of these folks work directly with us through the various ministries we worked with the years we were in South Africa.

One young lady, I'll call her C, who came over to work with us for two years, came first as a leader of one of those American basketball teams. We would lodge these teams in a particular sports team hostel while they were with us in Cape Town. Now, you have to understand the crime rate and criminal activity in South Africa is some of the highest in the world. So we would always do an orientation with our teams and help them understand this, and talked about things like staying in a group, not venturing out on your own, always be aware of your surroundings, and the like.

One night at the hostel, after C's team had come in from a long day of ministry and had finally gotten to bed, this fearless lady leader started hearing noises. The rooms her team were staying in were on the second floor, and the floors were hardwood. There was a door on the ground level, and then you ascended a flight of stairs to get to their rooms. Well, C heard what she decided were footsteps of someone coming up the steps and into the common area between their rooms. She was the leader of this group of high school basketball players so she had to protect them. The first thing she did was to make sure her door was locked. Then, she woke up her roommate to let her know what was going on, scaring this young girl half to death. What were they going to do? By the way, cell phones were not here yet so they were not an option at that point in time!

C looked around for a weapon, and found a flashlight shaped like a fish. That would have to do. Then, she decided that might not stop an intruder, especially when he had a gun. What else could she do? There was a window in the room that opened out onto the street, two stories below. Understand also that the street below was outside the hostel complex, outside the safety of the hostel security guard. C decided the best thing to do was to go out that window and run around to the gate and notify the security guard about the intruder she left in her loft with her basketball team. That was the plan, but how does she get down to street level from a second story window? Sheets! Tie the sheets together like she has seen on TV. So, that's what they did. C went out the window, broke the light on the side of the building in the process, climbed down the sheets to the street below and ran around the building to find the security guard, without getting shot in the process.

She and the guard went to the door, up the stairs,

looked through every room, waking up all the players who had no idea what was going on. Then, there was the noise again! What was it? The guard listened and then informed C that the noise was on the other side of the interior wall, other people walking up their steps to their rooms so they could go to bed, too.

C did not want to tell me about their night's activity the next day. But, her honesty got the best of her and she laid it all out for us, starting it off by saying, "Well, I guess I need to tell you what I did last night." I guess she thought I would think she was some nutcase. At least she was an honest nutcase who would go down protecting her players!

"This is how we know what love is: Jesus Christ laid down his life for us. And we ought to lay down our lives for our brothers and sisters." 1 John 3:16

"Greater love has no one than this: to lay down one's life for one's friends." John 15:13

C became a great friend to our family and it worked out great when she came back to Cape Town to work with us for two years. We all liked it so well that she went home and signed up for another two years.

Fireworks!

When the American basketball teams would come over, in addition to the tournament, we would take them around the Cape and conduct clinics in schools and communities. We worked with all culture groups in all kinds of areas. One day we had driven down to one of the more dangerous areas of Mitchells Plain because some business owners wanted us to do a clinic with kids in their community.

When we drove up, we got out of the vehicles and were talking about eating lunch before we set up the portable basketball goals. All of a sudden, we heard what sounded like fireworks, and some from the team were asking why fireworks would be going off. The other missionary and I looked at each other and knew those weren't fireworks, they were multiple gun shots.

The business owners ran out of their shops and gathered our group into their shops and lowered the metal garage doors over the windows. In the meantime, two gangs were shooting at each other in the park next door where the basketball clinic was to take place. A few minutes later, we could see through gaps in the doors that the police had arrived and the gangs had run away. So, the businessmen raised the doors and were open for business again, just like a normal day in the neighborhood.

Except, for us, this was not normal. Some of our USA team members were in shock and we weren't going to be able to stay for a clinic, we had to get them out of the area so they could cool off, which they were able to do so we could get back to work the next day. *(Dangerous Nuts!)*

Speaking of Gangs . . .

Another day we had gone to a township area where we were going to do a basketball clinic in the community with a group of youth that another friend from the Seminary had been working with. He wanted us to come and introduce basketball to the youth and to also share our faith with them.

When we drove up on the bus, this guy came onto the bus and shared some things with me which I, in turn, had to share with the team. I told them that this area was home to some pretty rough gangs, so for our guys who had ear rings in their ears, please take them out now. The reason for this was that each gang in the area had their "colors." Sometimes it was literally clothing of a certain color, and sometimes this included caps worn a certain way, or clothing arranged a certain way, or ear rings or other piercings worn in various parts of the body. Depending on what type of ear ring they wore and where that ear ring was located designated which gang they belonged to, and we didn't want to belong to any of them on that day!

One of our team members looked like he might object to taking his ear ring out, so I went ahead and informed him of this information. You can leave them in if you want, but those are the reasons why we think you should take them out. If you don't, this is how it's going to go down. We are getting off the bus and going to that court over there and leading a clinic. You are getting off the bus and going to that other court down there, because when they start shooting at

you, we won't be around.   He took out his ear rings
and played with the rest of us.   *(Basketball Nut!)*

Seal Island

We would take the American teams around for some sightseeing as well while they were in Cape Town. One day I was going to take them on a boat which took us out of the bay and around the point to see Seal Island where hundreds of seals lived. One of the basketball girls said she didn't want to go because she got seasick. I explained to her this was a pretty large boat and there were not really any waves to speak of in this part of the ocean. She still didn't want to go. I kept telling her this is a big boat, she wouldn't get sick on this boat, trust me. So, she finally got on the boat and we headed for Seal Island. Just out of the harbor, I looked around for Vange, and she was already spread eagle on one of the lounge areas of the boat! We asked her what was wrong but she could only grunt. I think she was seasick. Oh, come on.

When the boat got to the island we tried to get her to get up and take some pictures but she only grunted and handed someone her camera. When the boat finally got back into the harbor and docked, we were all walking off and the Captain of the boat was standing there shaking hands and saying goodbye to everyone. When Vange managed to get up and walk off the boat, he shook her hand and said he hoped she had a good voyage. Her response was something like this, "Are you serious? I hate your boat and I hated riding on it, thank you!" and walked away. The Captain looked at me and said, "Seasick, huh?" I nodded my head. *(Nuts!)*

Deep Sea Fishing

So, I guess now is as good a time as any to tell my fishing story. When it was getting time for our son to leave South Africa and go back to the USA for university, I wanted to do a father and son event. I had always wanted to go deep sea fishing but it was too expensive. One day, another friend told me he had organized a fishing trip and had two extra spaces on the boat, would I like to go and take Braden? That was going to be great, plus I didn't have to pay for it!

We met at Hout Bay Harbor one morning at 6:00 a.m. and got on a little fishing boat and headed out to sea. I asked where we were going and the Captain said the fish were about 40 miles out. Wow, I couldn't believe there were no fish any closer, all that water. But, we went 40 miles out to sea, riding up one wave and crashing down on the next, riding up one wave and crashing down on the next, wave after wave after wave. We passed the last lighthouse at Cape Point on our way out to sea. This is the area where the Indian and the Atlantic Oceans come together. This is the area where, years ago, sailing ships went down due to the turbulent seas and bad currents. Our boat was bucking around so much we just had to stand and hold on. We couldn't sit down or we'd be thrown out of the seat. I was beginning not to feel good about this day.

When we finally arrived at the spot, 40 miles out, they began preparing the lines. Well, let me tell you about the sea at that point. At one moment, you could look out and see the wave standing much higher than our boat. Then, the next moment, you could look out and see the water way below our boat because we were up on top of the wave. And we rolled and rolled like that all day long. And the more we rolled, the more seasick I became. I had been out in boats all my life, and had never been seasick. "They" say to just look at the horizon and you won't get sick. Let me tell you, there was no horizon, just waves going up and coming down, going up and coming down, you get the picture.

There were six of us on our boat, and I was the first to get sick. I won't explain that feeling to you nor will I tell you what I went through over the next few hours. At one point, I saw a container ship coming toward us in the distance. It got closer and I asked the Captain if he saw the ship. He said yes, we were in the shipping channel. Well, the ship got closer. I asked the Captain if we were going to get out of the shipping channel. "Yeah, soon," he replied. As that ship passed, I told the Captain that I would like to swim over to that ship and go wherever he was going, it couldn't be as bad as it was presently. He thought I was joking! *(Nut!)* Another time I thought that if they would contact the Coast Guard, I could throw myself overboard and give them a life rescue training exercise, they could rescue me and take me back to solid ground.

Needless to say, I didn't get in any fishing time that day. As a matter of fact, the fishing was so bad that they decided to go 10 more miles out to sea to see if there were any fish out there, so we did. There weren't.

By this time, Braden and the guy who asked us to go on this trip were seasick as well. Good. Not good for Braden, but the other guy! That friend may as well share my trip from "you know where." Our boat caught a total of one fish that whole day. The Captain summed up the day as a left-over from the storms we had the previous days.

Before we had left the dock that morning, he told me that it would be calm 40 miles out. Boy, was he wrong. As we headed back to the dock after just a really great day at sea, the Captain came over to me. Since he saw I was feeling a little better, he informed me that seasickness is something you think you're going to die from, but you won't. I told him I understood that to be very true. There you go, Braden, a fishing trip you will never forget! *(Nuts!)*

Basketball Association

As we worked with the basketball community in Cape Town, we got to know more of the folks who spent their time coaching and playing. I went to the annual meeting of the Western Cape Basketball Association one day so I could see what was going on and learn how they did things. At the end of the day, I walked out of there as the Chairman of that organization. Unexpected, to say the least. So, I found out real fast what goes on and how we did things. I served in that position for four years and met some great people along the way.

One day, someone from Basketball South Africa called to ask if I could meet Bill Laimbeer (former NBA player) at a hotel and take him to conduct a basketball clinic in one of our townships. Well, I didn't like Bill Laimbeer when he was playing in the NBA with the Detroit Pistons, some called him "the prince of darkness," but I figured I could take him to do this. When I got to the hotel, I was looking for a 6'11" white basketball player. Instead, this 6'11" black man came out to the vehicle and asked if I was looking for him. He introduced himself as Bob Lanier! BIG difference! I liked Bob Lanier, he had played for the Pistons and the Bucks. He had punched Bill Laimbeer one time in a game. So, we had a good time with that clinic. I asked him if he wanted me to get an interpreter and he asked me if these kids understood English. I told him they did but they might not understand him. He said he didn't need anyone to interpret and started talking with them and asking questions. They just looked at him with no response. After several attempts, he asked me again if they understood English. I told him they understood South African English, not his American slang, so we got an interpreter, and all went well. *(Really tall nut!)*

TV Basketball Commentators

With all the hype in American around the NBA and college basketball, South Africa was really pushing basketball as an exciting player and fan sport for all people. There was a TV sports channel that carried many of the games being played by the semi-pro league in the country.

When some of those games were going to be played in Cape Town, the producers decided to get 2 Americans to call the game on TV, I guess because basketball is known to be an American sport so they wanted American accents. So, they asked a friend of mine, Mike, who worked with Athletes in Action, and me to be the commentators for some of these games. I don't think they knew what they were getting into with us.

A few of the games we called live while the games were being played. We had a little computer screen in front of us to give us some stats to use while we commentated on the game. Most of the real stats we used were ones we were writing down as the games progressed. And we had to hold the microphones up against our mouth which was a bit uncomfortable and weird.

On one such game, we were going to call the game from the studio, because the game had already been played without commentary. They were going to replay it on TV with us commentating while we, too, were watching it on the screen. This should be interesting.

When we got into the studio with the large screen in front of us, they gave us a list of the teams. Now, you have to understand what we were faced with while commentating these games. These were African names being pronounced by Americans. As we were looking over that list, we knew there were going to be problems. So, we told the producer to let us know when it was time to start, in the meantime, we would be practicing these names.

So, Mike and I started going over the list of names. There were Ngomo, Nomsa, Motaung, Nteleti, Sethumba, Mtombo, Sebati, Shikwambo, Cronje, etc., etc., etc. We started laughing as we tried to pronounce the names, having fun with it, saying things like, "Hey, listen to this one, Chester Shikwambo!" "Listen to this one, Leslie Nteleti!" "Here's one, Frans Cronje!" The more we tried to pronounce them, the funnier it got. Then we tried to just get the starters correct so we could announce the starting lineups.

Well, back in the editing room, the producers were listening to all of this because the mics were live. One of the producers came out and whispered to us, "Just continue on, the audience must be loving this!" We were LIVE on the air! They thought it was so funny that they put us on the air prior to the game starting so the audience could listen to us practicing the names! How embarrassing. But, what a load of fun we had that day.

(Crazy basketball nut producers!)

VETS Basketball Tourney

I love playing basketball with people my own age, hence, I joined the VETS Basketball Club, where the men had to be over 35 and the women over 30. Every year they sponsored a national basketball tournament in a different part of the country. We had a friend, Z, from the old Yugoslavia, who played with us on our ISF team. Each year Z put together a team of guys from his old country who also lived in South Africa, and they had won this tournament for six years straight. He kept telling me to bring an American team over to give them some competition. So, one year I decided to do just that. I got together three of us Americans who lived in South Africa, and we invited five other guys from the USA to join us. We went to Durban, South Africa, that year to play in the national VETS tourney. Each time we got ready to play a team, we asked them if we could talk with them after the game. They would all agree, and after we beat them, excuse me, after we played them, we would sit down in a hallway or locker room and one of our players would share a testimony of how Jesus had changed his life and what it means to be a Christian.

It just so happened that the organizers thought it would be fun to put the Yugo team and the American team in the same double-elimination pool. So, after we beat the first two teams in our pool, we had to play the Yugo's. It was a very hard fought game, very physical as we knew it would be. At the last buzzer, we had beaten them by six points! And, boy, were they upset, first loss in six years. My friend who played on their team came over to me and told me he didn't think it was a good idea to talk right then, his players were pretty upset. So, we just had to leave because they would not speak to us. Well, to make the story great, that Yugo team went to the loser's bracket, won all their remaining games, and guess who we got to play in the Tournament's Championship Game? Yep, the Yugo's.

If we thought the first game was hard fought, this one was a barnburner. We had so many bruises on our bodies afterwards you would think we had been in a brawl. The score went back and forth, these guys were determined to beat this American team who had embarrassed them earlier. They knew the first game had to be a fluke. Plus, all the other teams in the tournament were there to watch the final game. Well, at the final buzzer there were ten points separating the teams, with the Americans on top. We had beat them again! And what happened next was just a God-thing. Z, my friend, came over to me, with all of his team, shaking our hands and congratulating us on the win. Z said they will listen to you now because they respect you. They felt the first time was a fluke, but the second win proved you're the better team today and they will talk. So, both teams sat down at mid-court since there were no games left to play, only the final Awards Banquet later that night.

One of our players stood and began to give his testimony of how Christ had changed his life and leads him each day. As he was speaking, all the other teams who had been sitting in the stands watching the game, saw what was taking place at mid-court. Those two teams who had battled so hard were now sitting together on the court. So, these teams came out of the stands and sat with us, and listened. It was a great time together and many questions came from many players. Some friendships had been forged during that tournament that we would build on over the next few years as we went back to the tournament in various cities around the country.

And, yes, I still cherish my gold medals!

(Still a basketball nut!)

Leadership Conference in the African Bush

Since I was the missionary Team Leader in Cape Town, I *got to go* to various leadership conferences over the years in various places around southern Africa. I don't remember there being an alternative to going. Anyway, one of these such conferences took place in Zimbabwe at a very remote river bush camp. There was not a fence around the camp, the camp was inside a wild animal preserve, hippos and crocodiles lived in the river, and everything else in the bush. We stayed in thatched roof rondavels (circular huts) with screens covering the windows, no glass. The doors were made of bamboo. Remember these building materials because you will recall them later in the story. To get to this location, we had to leave one of the vehicles, which was not four-wheel drive, in a small town while taking the other two four-wheel drive vehicles with us. We had about three too many guys for the vehicles, so those three went in a little motor boat up the river with a guide, while the vehicles began their trek through the bush. I was in one of the vehicles. We drove along a barely noticeable path, weaving between trees and plowing through dry river beds. We got stuck in one of the river beds and had to bring tree limbs over to put under the tires to get the vehicles out of the sand. It took almost two hours to finally get to the bush camp. The boat was already there, not much traffic on the river, just had to dodge the hippos.

There were two of us in each rondavel. There was a bush kitchen, and an outdoor dining area consisting of a long wooden table with chairs under the trees, surrounded by a half-circle wall of poles stuck in the ground, leaving one side open, with the river in the distance. Did I mention there was not a fence around this camp? One night as we were eating, we heard a noise on the other side of the pole wall. A mother elephant and her baby came walking past on the open side of our dining area. Gratefully, she walked on by and didn't stop to look around, she was on a mission to protect her baby.

We had a hunter with a big gun and a river guide with us for the week. They would be teaching us some things about the bush and the river. The hunter told a story one night about what to do if you walk up on a herd of mother elephants with babies or a herd of water buffalos. He said if you're in danger of elephants, quietly move away so they can't see you, as their eyesight is not so good. If you're in danger of the buffalo, climb the nearest tree. Don't climb the tree to get away from the elephant, he or she will knock it down. Then, he told a story of how the buffalo bulls protect the herd. He said that when danger comes to the herd, the main bull buffalo, who has been watching for trouble, comes out of the herd. Then, the other bull buffalos come out of the herd and line up behind him. They walk in a line toward the danger. If they need to deal with it, they will, or if the danger backs away, they turn around and go back to the herd. Now, here I am along with Nut Magnet #1, sitting there wondering and asking how would the hunter know that, and how did he know what a buffalo was thinking?

The next day we would decide whether we wanted to

go on a game walk or a canoe trip on the river. I asked if it was safe to go on the river in a canoe, since the hippos and crocodiles were in there. The river guide said, oh, sure it will be safe, he will be with that group and teach them how to do it. I told that group they were foolish to go on the river in a canoe. Remember that warning later.

The next day, I went with the group on the walk with the hunter with the big gun. Another smaller group went on the river with the guide, no gun. We walked along a trail through the bush, along the river, through some grasslands. We came around a bend of the river and noticed a herd of buffalo grazing on the grass beside the river. The hunter said for us to watch what happened next. He turned around and gave his gun to one of the missionaries, and then he jumped down off the trail about five feet to the grassy area. He began walking toward the herd of buffalo. When he got a little closer to them, we could see the largest bull lift his head and watch the hunter. That bull walked to the edge of the herd and stopped. Then, the other buffalo bulls walked out of the herd and lined up behind the main bull. Then, they all began walking toward the hunter. Again, amazing! I guess he did know what the buffalo were thinking after all! He turned and knelt down so they couldn't see him any longer. The large bull stopped and looked around, didn't see danger any longer, and they all turned around and went back to the herd.

We got back on the path and walked around another bend to find ourselves right in the middle of a herd of elephants with their babies. There were plenty of trees but not a good idea to climb those. So, we quietly removed ourselves from the area, and walked back to the camp without further sightings.

When we got back to the camp, the other group of missionaries were sitting around the campfire drinking coffee, wrapped in towels. When we asked what was going on, their response was a story which was almost unbelievable.

They went out in three canoes – the guide and one man in one canoe, two other men in one canoe, and three men in another canoe. The guide had explained to them to stay close and not to wander into the hippo pools. Evidently, while they were along the far side of the river, the canoe with three men got caught in the current and began to drift into a hippo pool area. The guide shouted at them to paddle out of there, but it was too late. A large hippo came up under their canoe and lifted it out of the water about three feet, flipping it over and throwing all three men into the water with the hippo. They said they were scrambling to try to get up on the overturned canoe to get out of the water. But, obviously, it was impossible for all three men to get onto the canoe.

The guide quickly took his canoe and the second canoe to what he thought was the river bank, but was actually a small island. He left those men there so he could take his canoe to rescue the three men in the water. When the men realized they were actually on an island, and noticed more hippos on the other side, they asked the guide what to do. He threw them a flare and said, "If a hippo comes to you, light the flare and put it in his mouth!" *Right.* The guide then paddled over to the men in the water and got them into his canoe. They said they didn't see that particular hippo again, guess the commotion scared him as much as it did them! For the record, hippos are responsible for more human deaths in Africa each year than any other animal.

Well, at first we thought these guys might be trying to pull a fast one over us. So, they took us over to the canoes and showed us the canoe that flipped over. There was about a ten inch by two inch gash in the bottom of the canoe where the hippo's tusk came through the canoe when he lifted it out of the water. I took a photo of that and have it on my computer today. We believed their story after that, but my remark about foolishness came back to me.

If this were the end of the bush story, that would be fine, but it's not. The last night, we were asking the hunter about dangerous situations he had faced over the years. He said he wanted to tell us a story about an instance that had happened at this very camp, but wanted to wait until the last night to tell it. *Great!*

One of his friends had been the hunter with a group of people who were staying in our same rondavels. One night, in one of the rondavels, there was what the men inside thought was a knock on the door. A young man got up out of his bed to see who was at the door. When he looked out a crack, he saw a lion trying to open the door. He pushed against the door to keep the lion out and yelled for his roommate to get up, a lion was trying to get in the door.

Understandably, the roommate thought he was making this up, so he wouldn't get out of his bed. And, then, the pressure on the door released, so the man thought the lion had moved on. As soon as he got back into bed, there was a noise in the bathroom. The lion had come through the screen window into the room where the men were in their beds. The lion started to paw at the roommate's feet and he started to scream for help. The man who had already seen the lion earlier had a large knife beside his bed so he threw it to his roommate for him to fend off the lion. The hunter and others had heard the commotion and screaming and came to the rescue. The hunter came into the room and shot the lion dead. After the story, our hunter said, "Okay, time to go to bed, have a good night's sleep." *Are you serious? (Nut-cake)*

Well, needless to say, some of us didn't get much sleep that night. My bed was beside the large screened window, and I heard everything that night. Late into the night, after I had drifted off to sleep, a noise outside my window woke me up. I heard a growling noise right outside my window and it scared me badly. I tried not to breath so whatever was out there wouldn't know I was in there. We had no knives, no cell phones that worked in the bush, and the hunter was in another rondavel across camp. I don't know what I did the rest of the night, but eventually the noise stopped, I got some sleep, and morning came.

At breakfast, one of the other missionaries in another rondavel asked me if I heard anything outside my window last night. I told them my story of the noise, and he said he heard it as well, and looked out and saw what it was. There was an elephant outside my rondavel scratching his bum on the wall beside the window. I asked the hunter what was the growling noise, and he told us that an elephant's stomach growls and it sounds just like the low growl of a lion. *Just get me out of this bush camp, please. (Nut elephant!)*

Is it over yet? On, no. Then, we had to draw straws to see who had to ride in the boat up the hippo and crocodile infested river to the extra vehicle, while the others made it out in the 4x4's. You guessed it, I drew a short straw! I had to ride with a couple others in the boat for about an hour. While traveling up the river, we could see the hippos and crocs along the way. Once, the motor quit and we started to drift. A hippo came up out of the water and looked at us. I looked around and saw that the driver was just changing the hose from the empty gas can to the full one. That's good.

Later in the trip, we were going slowly through a grassy spot in the river and the motor quit again, but we had gas. I asked the driver what the problem was and he said there must be grass wrapped around the propeller. *Well, I'm not going in to remove it, sorry.* But, he brought the motor up out of the water to where he could get to the propeller and remove the grass. I'm not sure how many hippos stuck their heads out of the water to see what was going on, I was just willing the driver to hurry and get us going again. Not my favorite time on the river. *(Nut, skipper!)*

Needless to say, our missionary leader decided not to

take another group to that particular bush camp any more. Later we heard from the hunter, who heard from the camp caretaker, that a pride of lions came into the camp the day after we left and laid around there all day before moving on. *Can't believe we missed the cats!*

6 OTHER COUNTRY TRAVELS

Botswana – Not Another Fishing Trip!

When Kaylan matriculated (graduated) from Pinelands High School, and we were in the process of finding a ministry position back in the USA, we decided to take the family on a final African safari. We traveled up to Botswana and near the border of Zambia and Zimbabwe at Victoria Falls. We stayed in a safari resort on the Chobe River, which runs into the Zambesi River which goes over the Victoria Falls further down.

One day I wanted to take Kaylan on a fishing trip since Braden and I had gone on a fishing trip a year or so earlier. We decided that since it was on a river and not the ocean, no one would get seasick. So, Kaylan, Braden and I went fishing in a small boat with a local fisherman. We would be trying to catch the famous tiger fish which lived in that area, a silver fish with some orange coloring and large, very sharp teeth.

The fisherman took us to a part of the river which was moving pretty good and had a small area of rocks in the middle where we stopped with the boat. He told us that this would be a good spot to try to catch the fish. About the time he stopped talking, a hippo stuck his head up beside the boat and looked at us, like we had disrupted his space. At the same time, another hippo on the other side of the boat stuck his head out of the water to see who was hogging their space. I took a picture of that hippo and in the picture you can see a rock just past the hippo's head with a large crocodile sunning himself. I looked at Kaylan and her eyes were really large as she asked the question, "Surely we're not fishing here, are we?" I looked at the fisherman and he said, "Well, maybe this is not such a good spot, we'll try another place." We were all satisfied with that answer. (Are you nuts?)

We found another spot, out of the fast water, and fished for a couple of hours. I ended up catching the only 3 tiger fish of the day, Braden and Kaylan had bites but never got them to the boat. We have some good photos of our fish with their tiger teeth. We gave the fish to the fisherman who said he had friends who liked to eat that kind of fish. So, we got back to the hotel safely, no seasickness, very sunburned, and with a great story to tell. And someone else enjoyed a meal of tiger fish that night!

Mauritius Anniversary!

There is a wonderful vacation destination about 1,200 miles off the southeast coast of the African continent called Mauritius. It is an island of 788 square miles in the Indian Ocean. It was the only home of the Dodo bird which became extinct, even though we looked everywhere for them while we were there!

For our 25th wedding anniversary, Karen and I decided to go for a week to Mauritius. We had some missionary friends who lived on Mauritius who were in the USA on furlough, so we could use their vehicle while there. When the kids learned of this plan, they said we needed to take them along as well. They said to get them their own room and we would never see them. Well, we did that, but somehow we saw them every day! And, had a great time as a family on the island, staying at a place called Flic en Flac.

We had reserved a 4-star resort on the beach. Several weeks before we left, the resort called and said there was construction going on at the resort, could they upgrade us to the 5-star resort next door, no extra charge. Well, I guess. It was very nice with meals provided. And, with the vehicle, we could go to the local market and buy snacks and sodas and not have to pay the high prices at the resort.

One day we went on an catamaran excursion. For the price of the excursion, everything was provided including snorkeling gear and snacks. The sodas at the resort were so high that we wouldn't buy them so when we got on the catamaran, they were FREE. We all had our share.

My son and I were not so sure about the snorkeling out in the middle of the Indian Ocean near a reef. We'd heard all the shark stories. But, we tried it anyway. When we got in the water and looked down at all the beautifully-colored fish along the reef, all of a sudden they turned and came toward us like they were in attack mode. Braden's eyes looked huge through that mask, like he was looking at another feared baboon! It was pretty frightening for a moment until we realized the guys on the boat were throwing bread into the water to attract the fish. *(Deckhand nuts!)*

Australia, New Zealand, Hawaii

When we would go on furlough to the USA for a time of visiting family and speaking about the work, the Board would provide the expenses for the trip. As we were preparing to go on furlough in 2000, we knew the Olympics were going to be in Sydney, Australia. We took what the Board would pay for a straight shot round trip to and from the USA, added an amount to that, and bought around-the-world tickets for the family.

We flew to Sydney and spent a week in a guest house, enjoying the Olympic activities and a few games. We had met the Principal of the Baptist Seminary in Sydney when he was teaching at our Cape Town Baptist Seminary. He told us that they would be out of the country at that time so we could use their car for the week, so it turned out to be very economical for us. Plus, when the owner of the guest house found out we were missionaries serving in South Africa, he didn't charge us anything for the use of the guest house.
(Very hospitable, caring nuts!)

We flew from Australia to New Zealand and spent a night there. We left New Zealand to fly to Hawaii where we would spend another week. This flight really confused our kids because we left New Zealand at one time, flew approximately 15-18 hours, and landed in Hawaii before we left New Zealand! New Zealand time zone is about 24 hours ahead of the USA west coast so it really confuses travelers.

We enjoyed Hawaii for a week and then flew through Los Angeles and on to Atlanta where we were met by both sets of parents.

Other Country Travels

While living in South Africa, we traveled to several other countries in Africa: Botswana, Lesotho, Swaziland, Zimbabwe, Zambia, and Kenya. And, of course, I have a story from each of these, but will save most of those for another time.

As we flew back and forth from the USA, we also traveled through the Netherlands, England, Switzerland, and Germany. During many of those trips we would either have or take a long layover, sometimes over three days, in order to explore areas in those countries.

Those travels helped our children develop a great world view. It seems odd today when we meet people from the USA who have never even traveled far from their hometown, much less to other states or around the world. It was definitely an adventure that none of us would trade.

Ron Lomax

CONCLUSION

Our family had a great life in South Africa for 18½ years. Sure there were some times that were tougher than others and we missed our families and friends back in the USA. We met some great people, developed some great friendships, and had some great experiences. Of course, we also met a few not so great people and had a few not so great experiences. But, that was home to our kids and they will tell you they are better today for that experience. That was home as they knew it. Karen and I knew life in America beforehand, but they grew up overseas.

We're grateful for the missionary experience in South Africa. We're grateful for how our churches in the Southern Baptist Convention supported us and took care of our needs and ministry budgets through giving to the Cooperative Program and Lottie Moon Christmas Offering. We're grateful for other friends and churches who also supported us through prayer as well as giving special gifts to make it possible to do some things our mission budget wouldn't cover.

Would we do it again? Who knows? We follow the Lord along the path He lays out for us. What we knew as a lifestyle then has changed and time has moved on. People have moved on. Mission Board policies have changed! It would never be the same or how we remember it.

We'll just continue to follow Him wherever He leads and cherish those memories. If that path is back to another land one day, hey, bring it on!

"I will instruct you and teach you in the way you should go; I will counsel you with my loving eye on you."
Psalm 32:8

"'For I know the plans I have for you,' declares the Lord, 'plans to prosper you and not to harm you, plans to give you hope and a future. Then you will call upon me and come and pray to me, and I will listen to you. You will seek me and find me when you seek me with all your heart.'"
Jeremiah 29:11-13.

God has a plan for your life too! His plan is designed *"to give you hope and a future,"* both immediately and eternally. It doesn't matter what has happened, better things are coming. That is your real and living hope!

You need to put your trust and hope in Jesus Christ:

Admit to God that you are a sinner. Repent, turning away from your sin. *Romans 3:23; 6:23*

Believe that Jesus is God's Son and accept God's free gift of forgiveness from sin, His salvation for you. *John 3:16; Romans 5:8; Ephesians 2:8-9*

Confess your faith in Jesus Christ as Savior and Lord and invite Him into your heart. *Romans 10:9-10, 13*

Then, go and share this news with a Christian leader! Find a place of Christian worship and Bible Study, and get involved!

Ron Lomax

ABOUT THE AUTHOR

Ron grew up on a cattle and crop farm in southeast Missouri. Karen grew up in Marietta, Georgia. They met in Ridgecrest, North Carolina, in 1977, and married in 1978.

Ron and Karen live in northwest Arkansas, having moved there at the end of 2011 from O'Fallon, MO, where Ron was Global Missions Pastor at First Baptist Church for 5½ years. Prior to that, they served as missionaries in South Africa with the International Mission Board, SBC, for almost 19 years. Ron currently serves as the Director of Missions at the Washington Madison Baptist Association in Fayetteville, AR. Ron and Karen have three married adult children, a couple of dogs, and a various assortment of granddogs!

Since seminary, Ron has served churches in Georgia & Missouri, and served churches, associations, and conventions in South Africa. He received his Bachelor of Science degree in Business Administration from Southeast Missouri State University and Master of Religious Education degree from New Orleans Baptist Theological Seminary. The Lomax's are becoming Razorback fans, but the Mizzou Tigers still rank a close second!

Made in the USA
Monee, IL
26 January 2022